The Ballymuckmore Bog Rocket

A Potcheen Powered Adventure

A Novel By

STEVEN HOOPER

Disclaimer: Buckle Up for Ballymuckmore!

While whispers of Ballymuckmore and its boggy charm might dance around real-life Ireland, any resemblance between this fantastical tale and... well, reality is purely coincidental. Yes, there are bogs in Ireland, and yes, they're quite fascinating (in a muddy, fascinating way), but this tale is a whimsical blend of truth-inspired settings and pure, unadulterated nonsense, seasoned with a generous helping of laughter, spuds and a lot of characters and livestock called Seamus.

Enjoy the ride, and remember, the only truth in this tale is the one you create in your heart. And like a good pot of potcheen, it's best enjoyed with a pinch of disbelief and a whole lot of imagination.

Slàinte Mhaith! (Cheers!)

Index

A Bog Full of Dreams 5
From the Ashes 16
Spudnik Weather Station 20
Masterminds 25
Spud Fields and Stolen Smiles 31
Unlikely Alliance 35
Galway Boy 42
Nuns on the Run 46
Bonanza is reborn 55
Wool and Wanderlust 62
Ten Paces 65
Zorg 69
Leaky's Luminous Mind 73
Of Kings and Legends 77
Love Blossoms in the Spud Fields 84
Skeptic Tanks 90
Sabotage 95
Stargazing and Stardust Dreams 101
Push Comes to Shove 106
Rattlin' Bog 111
Alien Encounters 118
Operation Spudzilla 122
Satin Skies 130
Fun Thing, Bunting 135
Loaves and Fishes 141
City Lights 147
Bog Crater 153
Customs Still Searching 157
Day of Reckoning 161
Blessed be Spudnik 165
Are Ewe Dancing 168

Fly Spudnik, Fly 172
Epilogue 180

A Bog Full of Dreams

If it hadn't been the Pub with No Name, it would have been called something else.

Deep in the heart of Ireland, nestled amidst rolling hills and fields like an emerald brooch on a tweed waistcoat, lies Ballymuckmore. Don't bother reaching for your fancy atlas, for Ballymuckmore doesn't like to boast. It prefers the anonymity of a whispered ballad, a sheepdog's knowing bark, or the scent of peat smoke curling from a chimney on a wind-whipped evening.
Life in Ballymuckmore hums to a slow, ancient rhythm. Mornings are painted with the milky light of dawn, chased away by the bark of Seamus, the ever-philosophical sheepdog, and punctuated by the rhythmic clinking of pails as Biddy O'Rourke milks her beloved flock. Days stretch like lazy cats in the sun, filled with the murmur of gossip carried on the breeze, the clatter of boots in the Pub with No Name, and the gentle hum of Seamus's tail thumping against the floorboards.

But beneath the sleepy surface, an undercurrent of mischief bubbles like Leaky's infamous brew, given many names, Irish Moonshine, Mountain Dew, but known throughout Ireland as poitin. An art form in its own right, turning knurly old potatoes into a silky smooth (Leaky wishes) alcoholic delight.

At this point in our tale of, well, I wont spoil it, but I feel I must apologise. My editor has insisted that I use the anglicised pronunciation of potcheen, which apparently will be better understood by the masses. For this I am sincerely sorry.

While we're at it, for those unfamiliar with Irish pronunciations, Aoife is pronounced, 'Eefa'. You'll meet her very soon and it will make reading the tale a lot easier. Now, enough of the Gaelic lessons, let's get on with the story.

Ballymuckmore harbours a secret: a community woven together not just by shared potatoes and sheep, but by an insatiable thirst for stories, a twinkle in the eye that says, "I've seen things, and I'm not telling." . Where dreams are brewed stronger than the potcheen, and laughter echoes louder than a flock of startled sheep.

And smack dab in the middle of it all is the Pub with No Name, the Holy Grail of gossip and the Black Hole of sobriety. So christened due to a long-forgotten disagreement over a stolen pig and a hastily poured pint, it's the beating heart of this secret society, where every whispered dream and outlandish scheme finds a home, alongside the occasional lost sock and forgotten dignity. Its floorboards, worn smooth by countless boots and spilled pints, have witnessed births, wakes, and everything in between. And those walls, adorned with newspaper clippings older than the barkeep's jokes, wear the secrets of the village like well-loved hats. Pull up a stool, listen to the whispers carried on the smoke, and let Ballymuckmore weave its magic upon you. We're on the cusp of something grand, and it all begins, as any good legend should, in the heart of the Pub.

Every Saturday, around the time the church bells finished their gossipy chiming, a ragtag quartet would claim their throne at the splintered oak table in the corner, their arrival as regular as the tide and their spirit just as unstoppable

First came Finbar "Finny" McGillicuddy, a whirlwind of tousled hair and mischief, slid into the booth with a wink at Agnes, his charm as potent as the aroma of her sausages and white pudding.

"Full Irish all round, if you please Agnes, and an extra banger for Seamus," he declared, his voice tinged with the lilt of the bog.

Siobhán "Sheebie" O'Rourke, Finny's childhood friend, followed shortly after. A sharp-tongued shepherdess with eyes as deep and as dark as the bog and a smile that could coax a smile from a stone, she entered with a swagger, accompanied, as always, by Seamus, her trusty sheepdog. Her trusty shillelagh, polished to a dark gleam, leaned against the table, a silent extension of her fiery spirit.

Liam "Leaky" O'Sullivan, the village tinkerer, unofficial philosopher and purveyor of all liquids Irish, stumbled in next, his face etched with the map of past pints and untold stories. He sank into his seat, his pockets bulging with all manner of tools and a flask containing his latest liquid inspiration.

Dr. Aoife Maguire, the astrophysicist banished to the countryside by her stuffy colleagues, was the last to arrive. She waltzed in, fresh as a daisy, cute as a button and as sharp as a tack. Her fiery red hair pulled back in a practical braid, her eyes as green as emeralds, she perched on the edge of the bench, scanning the room with a practiced eye. But beneath the scientist's gaze, a secret warmth flickered, a shared joke with Finny, a lingering smile reserved for Leaky's outlandish pronouncements.

Here, the heroes aren't knights in shining armour, but this ragtag band of dreamers and doers, fuelled by ambition and spud-powered courage. They're the ones who keep this village from succumbing to dullness, injecting each day with a healthy dose of chaos and a sprinkle of delight.

But revealing too much would be like spoiling a good joke, wouldn't it? So, dear reader, settle in like a seasoned villager, for in Ballymuckmore, patience is not just a virtue, it's a survival skill.

Agnes, the formidable pub proprietress, ruled the house with a practiced hand. Her booming voice loud enough to wake the dead - or at least startle them into ordering a pint. Her assistant, Sean, a youth of the village with perpetually flour-dusted hair, scurried between tables, balancing precariously laden trays with the agility of a seasoned acrobat.

Their Full Irish breakfasts arrived with a flourish. Each plate was a culinary landscape, a mountain of golden fried eggs draped over plump sausages, rashers crisped to perfection, fried mushrooms, and potato creations ranging from crispy boxty to fluffy farls. Baked beans glistened like molten gemstones, while grilled tomatoes added a splash of vibrant colour. Toast, piled high and buttered generously, awaited its fate at the hands of the hungry ensemble.

Finny, as always, attacked his food with gusto, shovelling forkfuls into his mouth with a running commentary on the day's potential mischief. Aoife, ever the meticulous one, savoured each bite, dissecting her potato farl before enjoying it. Sheebie ate quietly, a contented smile gracing her lips as she relished the familiar flavours. Leaky, never far from his notebook, paused between bites, scribbling observations about the breakfast's nutritional value and the cultural significance of each ingredient.

Their conversations flowed like the endless mugs of tea Agnes kept refilling. They debated the merits of hurling strategies, the latest gossip (courtesy of Agnes' keen ear), and Leaky's latest scientific musings. Laughter erupted as Finny recounted a particularly outrageous prank, punctuated by Sheebie's gentle admonishments and Aoife's dry wit.

It wasn't just the food that fuelled them. It was the shared laughter, the comfortable silences, the unspoken bond that transcended words. In the haven of the Pub, among the chaos and laughter, they found not just nourishment for their bodies, but for their souls. The Full Irish Breakfast was more than just a meal; it was a ritual, a celebration of friendship, and a reminder that the best things in life were often found in the simplest moments, shared with good friends.

Aoife, sat back in her seat, her plate so clean it could go straight back in the cupboard. "Agnes has surpassed herself this morning." She remarked with a satisfied sigh.

"Magnificent" Leaky commented, sitting back and adjusting his belt.

Finny's plate resembled the aftermath of a particularly messy military campaign. Fried eggs, resembling more a sunny-side-up massacre, formed a moat around the crater left by vanished sausages. Beans, like rogue ammunition, had splattered across the surrounding territory, staining both plate and tabletop. Toast, once crisp and golden, now lay soggy and limp, casualties of overzealous buttering. A lone mushroom, miraculously intact, stood among the chaos, a lone brave soldier surveying the wreckage.

In short, Finny's plate was a battlefield where breakfast had been fought and, judging by the triumphant grin on his face, thoroughly enjoyed.

Finny removed the last remnants of breakfast from around his mouth, then pulled a sketch from his pocket which he slapped down on the table, avoiding the casualties of his breakfast.

"This, my friends, is the Spudnik Super Slinger! Imagine, potatoes raining down like celestial dew, impregnating the barren fields of County Cork!"
Aoife tried to maintain an air of academic detachment, but a smile tugged at the corner of her mouth. "Impregnating is it now?"
Sheebie snorted, "Spudnik Super Slinger? More like Crazy Cork Contraption!"
"Nay, nay," Leaky, who slouched next to Finny, his beard glistening with morning dew and the faintest whiff of potcheen, wagged a finger, "think of the possibilities! Spud shooting could replace Clay pigeon shooting as a national sport. "
Seamus let out a particularly expressive bark, tail thumping in approval.
Aoife, unable to resist any longer, chuckled, "Leaky, especially for you, that's not such a bad idea."
The pub was slowly coming alive. Biddy O'Rourke, her formidable bulk draped in a shawl as green as the bog itself, stomped in, muttering about errant sheep and the rising price of peat. Seamus, with a knowing look, trotted over to greet her with a wag of his tail and a nudge of his head towards the table. Biddy followed his gaze, a flicker of amusement lighting up her round face.
"Still at it, are you Finny? What fresh madness are you brewing this fine morning?"
Finny grinned, spreading his arms like a showman, "Biddy, my dear, prepare to be amazed! We shall not only reach the stars, but we shall nourish them with the finest spuds Ballymuckmore has to offer!"
Biddy snorted, the sound somewhere between a huff and a chuckle, "That I'd pay to see," she declared, sinking into a

chair next to Seamus, who promptly settled his head on her lap, earning a scratch behind the ears.

Sheebie, grinned. The sort of grin that spelt mischief. "So, Leaky, I hear there's a new moonbeam brightening your nights these days, eh? A lass from Ballyhubba, is it? Eyes as blue as the sky after a rainstorm, hair like spun sunshine?"

"Now, Sheebie, you know I wouldn't gossip…" Leaky mumbled while taking another mouthful of tea.

Finny, his grin trying to join his ears together, "Gossip? You call that gossip? We heard you mooning over her like a lovesick sheep at the spud harvest! Leaky McLovey, they're callin' you!"

They erupt in laughter, the clinking of mugs forming a joyful symphony. Leaky couldn't hide his blushes, but a spark of newfound confidence glinted in his eyes.

Aoife joined in,"Spill the beans, Leaky. Who is this mystery maiden stealing your focus from all things potato related?"

Leaky sighed, defeated, and smiled. "Morna's her name. She works at the Ballyhubba bakery, bakes the finest apple tarts this side of Tipperary. And her smile, well, it's enough to melt even the frostiest turnip."

"So it's true!" Sheebie sounded surprised "What magic spell has she used on you? Some leprechaun dust sprinkled over her crust perhaps."

Leaky, somewhat defensively, "Don't be daft, Sheebie. She's as down to earth as a freshly dug spud, but… there's somethin' special about her, like stardust sprinkled on her freckles."

"Stardust, eh? Sounds serious, lad. You got any plans to woo her over? Or are you going to keep mooning at her pies from afar?" Finny sees that maybe, just maybe, Leaky has found someone spuddle-brained enough to take him seriously.

"I… I was thinkin' about takin' her on a walk, maybe up to the Whispering Bog. Show her the hidden waterfall, tell her stories of infamous exploits."

"Now that's the Leaky we know! Forget the aliens and moonbeams, just be yourself. Your stories are better than any celestial conspiracy, anyway." Aoife offering words of encouragement.

"And be sure to bring along a potato pie or two, love-struck fool. Ballyhubba bread may be fine, but Ballymuckmore spuds reign supreme!" Sheebie added, always offering up good advice.

The Pub with No Name, usually a haven for tales of the unknown, had become a stage for a different kind of story – one of potato-powered romance and the quiet courage of a village dreamer.

And so, as the sun climbed higher, bathing the pub in a golden glow, the murmurs of conversations intertwined with the clatter of crockery and the laughter of friends. Saturday mornings in the Pub with No Name were a ritual, a tapestry woven from shared potatoes, whispered dreams, and the occasional splash of Leaky's "moonbeam-infused" potcheen. It was a haven for the eccentric, a launching pad for outlandish dreams, and the beating heart of Ballymuckmore, where even the spuds whispered of stardust and the most impossible notions found fertile ground.

Saturday had a routine that was the mainstay of their friendship.

Breakfast was always followed by a stroll along the edge of the bog to Leaky's sanctuary, the place where his dreams took flight and strange concoctions came into being.

"What have you got brewing for us today, Leaky?" Sheebie inquired, a hint of trepidation lacing her words. "This isn't going to be another one of those incidents like last week, is it?"
"Absolutely not," Leaky declared proudly. "And besides, your vision returned within a few minutes."
"I had tunnel vision for an hour!"
"Rest assured, I've tested this batch and it's one of my finest. The sheep showed no ill effects, although, one of them did become a little hoarse."
"Wow, that's clever" Finny chuckled.
"No, it just had a cough. There's nothing to worry about. You'll be good" Leaky tried to reassure Sheebie, although she remained unconvinced.

Welcome to Leaky's shed, where all things are possible, even if improbable. It would be hard to find a more ramshackle hut. Though, for all its faults, It was perfectly in tune with nature; the spiders helped reinforce the roof with their cobwebs and the mice recycled any morsel which found its way onto the floor.

The debate about Leaky's latest concoction raged on. Sheebie wrinkled her nose at the pungent fumes wafting from the still, "Lunar Lemming Liqueur? More like Swamp Scum Surprise!" Finny, eyes alight with the glow of inspiration, scribbled on a scrap of paper, oblivious to the growing tension. Aoife, ever the voice of reason, suggested, "Taste-Like-Muck might be a more honest starting point."
Leaky, beard twitching and eyes glazed with moonshine-induced reverie, declared, "Ah, but the name will come to me, like a whisper on the wind!"

But the only whispers in the shed were the ominous crackle of the fire and the hiss of escaping steam. In a far corner, a stray ember, unnoticed in the chaos, licked at a pile of dry hay. With each flicker, it grew more determined, its malevolent glow casting eerie shadows against the shed walls as it greedily sought out more fuel to feed its hungry flames. Like a red-eyed spectre in the darkness, it reached out its fiery fingers, grasping and consuming everything in its path, a silent threat lurking in the shadows, waiting to unleash its fiery fury upon the unsuspecting shed.

Laughter and arguments dissolved into a shared breath as acrid smoke filled their lungs. The flames, fed by the hay, danced around the neck of a discarded earthenware jug, still pregnant with the volatile vapours of Leaky's latest batch.

Sheebie coughed, eyes streaming, "Leaky, what in the holy bog-"

Her words were cut short by a deafening explosion. The jug, propelled by the fiery blast, became a missile of moonshine madness, a potcheen projectile, arcing across the shed and punching a jagged hole in the roof.

Through the newly minted skylight, they glimpsed the sun, momentarily stunned into silence. But the silence was shattered by the roar of flames, licking at the dry wood of the shed.

Panic seized them. Finny, papers scattering like frightened stars, stumbled towards the still, hands grasping for anything to stem the inferno. Sheebie, her pragmatism kicking in, grabbed a bucket and rushed to the nearby tap, water splashing in a desperate dance against the fire.

Aoife, eyes wide with fear, coughed through the thick smoke, searching for Leaky, who'd been thrown back by the blast. His glazed eyes met hers, a moment of shared terror before the smoke, heavy as a bog blanket, swallowed them whole.

The scene, moments ago one of merry chaos, was now a tableau of terror. The shed, a pyre spewing smoke and flame, held within its fiery embrace the fate of our unlikely heroes. As the flames danced higher, licking at the sky, one question hung heavy in the choking air: would dawn find them amongst the ashes, in which case this would be a very short story, or had their dreams gone up in smoke, consumed by Leaky's latest distilled blunder?

From the Ashes

Smoke still clung to the air like cobwebs, a ghostly reminder of the near-inferno. But among the smouldering hay and singed rafters, a different sound bloomed – the infectious laughter of Leaky, bubbling up like potcheen in a still. He peeked out from under a makeshift haystack, eyes as wide as dinner plates and beard singed black, chuckling maniacally.
"Did you see that, lads? Did you see it soar? My finest brew yet, propelled by celestial fury itself!"
One by one, the others emerged from their smoke-covered hiding places, coughing and blinking at the afternoon sky, now visible through the new, jagged skylight. Finny, his hair as wild as the smoke itself, grinned, a spark of an idea dancing in his eyes.
"Leaky, you glorious, moonshine-addled genius! That wasn't just any explosion, that was a prototype! A celestial catapult, fuelled by your potcheen dreams!"
Sheebie wiped soot from her nose and snorted. "Don't let Finny's half singed brain cloud your judgment, Leaky. It was a near-apocalypse, not a spaceship. You could have killed us all"
But Aoife, eyes gleaming with the first flicker of scientific excitement, interjected, "Actually, the trajectory of that jug… it was incredible! We should measure the distance, analyse the blast! This could be…"
"Spudnik Rocket Fuel 2.0?" Sheebie finished, sarcasm dripping from her voice.
"No, Sheebie," Finny countered, his voice firm with newfound purpose, "this is bigger than potcheen fireworks. This is the birth of the Spudnik Rocket!"

Finny expected the band of friends to be rolling around on the floor in fits of laughter, but nobody laughed. "I said Spudnik Rocket"
"We heard you" Aoife's thoughts were elsewhere.
Despite the lingering smoke and charred wood, a spark of hope crackled through the air. The near-disaster had inadvertently ignited a dream, a vision of rockets fuelled by Leaky's cosmic concoctions, crisscrossing the sky among the stars.
With soot-stained faces and singed eyebrows, they decided to call a halt to their moonshine testing. The shed, now sporting a skylight, could wait.
As they walked beside the darkening bog, the quietness grew deafening. Each of them alone with their own thoughts. They knew their lives were irrevocably changed.
Spudnik Rocket, for many years a whispered joke over pints, was now a tangible dream, fuelled by potcheen fumes, sheepish determination, and the unshakable spirit of Ballymuckmore, a village where even near-disasters could spark dreams that reached for the stars.

The Pub with No Name, bathed in the warm glow of its peat fire, beckoned with the promise of pints, gossip, and perhaps, just perhaps, the first scribbles of a blueprint for a potato-powered rocket, born from the ashes of Leaky's celestial-calibre brew.
The air in the Pub crackled with post-apocalyptic energy. Smoke still clung to their clothes, a faint scent of singed hay and Leaky's celestial-infused moonshine. Despite the near-death experience, their usual booth held them in a familiar embrace, the clinking of pints and murmur of gossip a soothing balm after the fiery chaos.

Finny, his hair as wild as the bog wind during a storm, was the first to speak, launching into his version of the events. "It was a rocket, I tell you! Leaky's finest concoction, propelled by the very breath of the cosmos!" His eyes sparkled with a mixture of relief and manic excitement, tracing the trajectory of the jug in the air with his finger.

Sheebie rolled her eyes. "Did that jug hit you in the head, Finny?It was a near-disaster, a moonshine-fuelled fireball." She took a swig of her Guinness, " and you're welcome by the way, for me putting it out, while you lot were running round like headless chickens".

Aoife, her brow furrowed in thought, tapped her notepad. "Yeah, thanks Sheebie, that was really quick thinking. But the trajectory… it was impressive, almost… controlled. We need to calculate the force, the weight of the jug…" Her voice trailed off, lost in the data dance swirling in her mind.

Sheebie shook her head in disbelief.

Leaky, his beard singed black and reeking of fumes, chuckled, a sound like pebbles rattling in a bog bucket. "Ah, lads, you don't understand! It was the spirits guiding it! My potcheen, moonshine with a shine for the moon, taking flight on wings of fire!"

The conversation became a cacophony of speculation, each telling their own tale of the fiery near-miss. Finny saw potato-powered rockets soaring through the cosmos, Sheebie imagined a sky full of flaming moonshine jugs hurtling towards them, and Aoife, ever the scientist, saw equations dancing in the smoke, the potential for propulsion a tantalising whisper on the wind.

Amidst the debate, the burning question needed an answer: "Could potcheen be used as rocket fuel?" They all looked towards Aoife.

"Ok, you want the sciencie bit. " Aoife paused, glancing around at their expectant faces, being the only true scientist amongst them. "Why not!"

"Why not." Finny looked puzzled. "All your university degrees and your best answer is 'Why not'!"

"Yeah, but I"m not saying we're just pourin' Leaky's brew straight into the tanks. No, that wouldn't do at all. We would need to refine it, but with a bit or work, why not.

Finny glanced at Sheebie and Leaky, who both grinned.

"Ok, looks like we have ourselves some home brewed rocket fuel"

But amidst the excitement, there's a shadow of worry. Biddy O'Rourke's nose is sharper than a sheepdog's teeth, and news of a potcheen-powered rocket reaching her would be faster than a rogue spud flying across the bog.

Sheebie whispers, her shillelagh tapping a silent rhythm on the table. "If we're going to do this, it needs to be just us. We can't be letting the rest of the village know what we're up to."

The other occupants of the booth nodded in agreement.

And so, as the fire crackled in the hearth and the night deepened outside, the seed of the Spudnik Rocket was firmly planted. Not in a sterile lab or a government-funded research facility, but in the smoky haven of the Pub with No Name, kindled by laughter, near-death experiences, and the boundless, potato-powered dreams of a group of friends from a village on the edge of the bog. The question of potcheen's fuel potential remained unanswered, but it had ignited a fire in their hearts, a fire that all the water in the bog couldn't extinguish.

Spudnik Weather Station

The sun, its mischievous grin like a guilty child peeking through a charred hole in Leaky's roof, cast long shadows across the aftermath of their near-fatal disaster. The air carried the lingering scent of singed hay and moonshine with a hint of otherworldly intrigue, but beneath the chaos, a new energy crackled like sparks from a wild bonfire, a hum of purposeful chaos.

Finny, perpetually smiling, whistled a jig as he tackled the mountain of debris. Old tires, their treads worn smooth by tales of midnight tractor races, tumbled out like forgotten dreams. Rusty cogs and tangled wires, veterans of countless contraptions and near-explosions, clinked like whispered stories. Each piece, encrusted with cobwebs and dust, held a memory, a testament to Leaky's boundless tinkering spirit and the team's collective knack for mischief.

And as Finny whistled his tune and the debris began to disappear, it was as if the shed itself whispered its approval, its dusty corners alive with the echoes of laughter and the promise of new adventures yet to come.

Sheebie, her gaze sharp as a sheepdog's, surveyed the chaos with a sigh. "This isn't just a shed, Finny," she muttered, hefting a dented helmet adorned with a mismatched pair of antlers. "This is Leaky's museum of mayhem, a shrine to every near-arrest and accidental invention."

Aoife paused before a stack of yellowed newspaper clippings. The headlines spoke of UFO sightings and inexplicable cow disappearances. A smile tugged at the corner of her lips, the scientist in her fascinated by the local superstitions.

Aoife starts leafing through one of the papers. "Still listening to those "Whispers from the Bog" broadcasts, Leaky? Heard any news from the lizard people lately?" she said with a smirk.
Leaky scoffs. "Don't be startin' with me, Aoife. Them reptilian rulers are real, and one day you'll see their scaly faces for yourself. How do you explain the crops circles in ..."
The friends knew each other so well, they could finish each other's sentences.
"Away wi' yer. You were totally spuddled, you couldn't stand up straight. The crop circles were Finny and Sheebie last week, dancing, well that's what they said it was, but I think its was your brew leading them astray."
Finny and Sheebie joined hands and started waltzing round the shed.
"Oh, yeah, you really were spuddled that night, even more than normal" Finny added.
Leaky searched around him, looking for something, anything to divert the attention away from himself, his eyes eventually resting on an old friend.
His beard still singed black and eyes twinkling with moonshine-tinged mischief, pulled a dented tin can from a pile of hay. "Ah, lads, look what I found! My very first still, the one that nearly sent Seamus soaring with the geese!"
Seamus, ever the stoic observer, thumped his tail at the mention of his near-flight, a silent testament to Leaky's creative mishaps. As the day unfolded, stories intertwined with discarded treasures. Rusty fishing rods whispered of midnight escapades to Farmer Brennan's pond, a dented bicycle helmet boasted of daredevil descents down Widow O'Toole's hill, and a collection of colourful rosettes winked at memories of summer fete competitions won and lost.

But over shadowing the laughter and reminiscing, their Rocket dream loomed ever large. Each salvaged piece, each whispered story, became a building block, a tangible reminder of their ambition. The hole in the roof, no longer a symbol of near-disaster, transformed into a window to the stars, a constant reminder of their celestial goal.
"I can't believe you kept these" Sheebie holding a homemade bow and a quiver of arrows. "Especially after you shot yer Da's prize cockerel. "
"I may have taken out that scrawny excuse for a chicken only because you lot couldn't hit the broad side of a barn," Leaky tried to defend himself, "But let's be real, it was only a prize winner because it was the only cockerel in Ballymuckmore."
"We were fashionably late for school a bit after that" Finny laughed.
"Look at us now" Sheebie smiled, "exploding jugs. We haven't learnt much , have we ?"
"Ballymuckmore Spud-keteers" Aoife held a sword aloft, another childhood memento.
"All for one and one for all" Their joined voices echoing around the piles of memories.
As night fell and the friends finished up for the evening, the shed, though far from pristine, felt like a haven of possibility. The rubble had been transformed into a foundation, the stories into fuel, and the camaraderie into an unshakable resolve. The Spudnik Rocket, born in the flames of a moonshine-fuelled explosion, had found its workshop, a place of memories, mischief, and dreams reaching for the stars.
As they walked beside the darkening bog, they recalled daring escapades from their childhoods, each one more incredible than the last. Each of the tales, without exception, had Sheebie, the girl who could give you a look that butter wouldn't melt in her

mouth, right bang in the middle of the chaos. A pattern was clearly emerging.

Their laughter continued as they reaped their reward for the endeavours of the day, tall glasses of Guinness. Sustenance well earned.

Sheebie's question hung heavy in the smoke-kissed air of the Pub with No Name, cutting through the usual cacophony like a well-aimed shillelagh. "How big are ya thinking this rocket is going to be, Finny?" she asked, her gaze fixed on the dreamer with a glint of challenge in her eyes.

Finny, perpetually lost in a universe of celestial potatoes, blinked as if returning from a moonshot daydream. "Big, Sheebie! Big enough to carry Fiona, a couple of spuds for good measure, and maybe Seamus, if he behaves himself."

Seamus, sprawled at Finny's feet, thumped his tail in agreement, a silent vote of confidence in his space faring potential.

Laughter rippled around the table. Aoife, her notebook resting open on her lap, chuckled, "Seamus in space? Can you imagine it?"

The question of size, however, lingered in the air.

Large enough to transport Seamus and a few of his charges was considerable. This was no firework and would most probably raise a few eyebrows (and pitchforks) among the more conservative residents of Ballymuckmore.

Leaky, usually brimming with lunacy, remained uncharacteristically quiet, swirling the dregs of his pint in his glass, as if searching for inspiration in the amber depths. Finally, he let out a guttural chuckle, sending a spray of Guinness across the table. "Why not the whole bog, lads? Imagine it! Ballymuckmore, a celestial spud, hurtling through the cosmos!"

"Really ?" Aoife was unimpressed with his suggestion.
The table erupted in a chorus of protests. Sheebie nearly choked on her tea, Finny spluttered about fuel efficiency, and Aoife scribbled furiously in her notebook, calculations dancing before her eyes.
The discussion veered from the practical (potato-powered engines with optional sidecar for sheep) to the fantastical (a rocket disguised as a giant leprechaun farting through the cosmos). But underneath the laughter and outlandish proposals, a seed had taken root.

Masterminds

Aoife surveyed the mismatched chairs scattered around Leaky's shed, each occupied by a crucial member of Spudnik's brain trust. Finny, as excited as a spring lamb, bounced in his seat, half a spud tucked behind his ear. Sheebie, ever the voice of reason, scribbled notes on a scrap of paper, her brow furrowed. And Leaky, as usual, resembled a mad professor amidst his collection of sprockets and gears, looking as if he were on the brink of a breakthrough or a breakdown – sometimes it was hard to tell which.

"Alright, lads and lass," Aoife began, her voice ringing out over the clinking of wrenches. "We all know the dream: Spudnik, a potcheen-powered potato soaring towards the stars. But before we even think about launch sequences, we need a design, a blueprint for our interstellar masterpiece."

Finny, unable to contain his enthusiasm, blurted out, "Imagine it, Aoife! A spud-shaped behemoth, soaring through the cosmos on a wave of potcheen fumes!"

Sheebie chuckled, her eyes twinkling. "Finny, love, while poetic, a spud-shaped rocket is more likely to resemble a mashed potato than a majestic spacecraft."

Leaky, finally untangling a bunch of wires, chimed in, "Think streamlined, lads! Lightweight metal construction is key. No hay and bog-wood, Finny, as tempting as it may be."

Aoife nodded, her eyes twinkling. "That's the Ballymuckmore spirit, Leaky! So where do we start?"

Sheebie grinned. "Remember Mrs. O'Leary's shed extension that went haywire last month? Heard she's offering scrap metal at a bargain price."

A collective groan filled the shed. Mrs. O'Leary's legendary temper was as well known as her questionable building skills.

"Fear not," Aoife winked, "your charm, Finny, can work wonders. A persuasive word and a promise of Seamus's lucky clover stew, and Mrs. O'Leary might just become an unlikely sponsor."

A lively discussion ensued, accompanied by mugs of strong tea and the occasional swig of "research potcheen" (strictly for quality control purposes, of course). They brainstormed ideas, discarding some as quickly as they surfaced.

"Old washing machines for the base?" Finny suggested, earning a skeptical look from Sheebie. "Too flimsy, Finny. We need something that can take the weight."

Leaky stroked his beard thoughtfully. "What about corrugated iron for the sides? Plenty of barns around that wouldn't miss a few sheets. Sturdy, lightweight, and readily available… with a little 'borrowing,' of course."

Finny, a spark igniting in his eyes, slammed his fist on the table. "What about the old bus graveyard? Those wrecks are chock-full of metal, and nobody's missing a rusty panel or two."

"And a roof, or six," Sheebie added, "There's enough sheet metal there to cover at least half the rocket."

Aoife grinned. "Finny, you're a genius! And the aluminium roofs on some of those barns… imagine the gleam of Spudnik reflecting the moonlight!"

The plan was coming together, not spud shaped as Finny had hoped, but Ballymuckmore shape.

"But what about the fuel tank?" Sheebie asked, her practical mind already worrying about safety. " potcheen is potent, remember?"

"It needs to be large enough to hold thousands of litres of the magic liquid." Aoife had a worried look on her face. "That is going to take some serious 'borrowing'".

Hours melted away as they sketched, debated, and laughed. Ideas bounced around like sheepdogs chasing rabbits, slowly coalescing into a cohesive plan. Spudnik would be a marvel of ingenuity, a patchwork quilt of salvaged materials and unwavering Ballymuckmore spirit. It would be a testament to their dreams, fuelled by potcheen and held together by determination and good humour.

Having exhausted both themselves and the well of ideas they were pulling from, greater sustenance was needed than the snacks, and that's being generous to describe them as snacks, that could be found around Leaky's shed.

The Pub with No Name, usually a haven for tall tales and drunken dreams, had become their refuelling station. Its worn floorboards now resonated with the whispers of engineers, its fire casting flickering shadows that danced like stardust on the walls. For in Ballymuckmore, even the most outlandish dreams can find fertile ground, stirred by laughter, Guinness, and a shared potato pie.

However, Ballymuckmore, a village where gossip flowed like the bog river and secrets thrived like sheep in clover, had grown restless. The sight of Finny sketching on napkins, Aoife poring over thick books, and Sheebie wielding a tape measure with suspiciously shifty eyes, had tongues wagging faster than a sheepdog chasing its tail.

Michael Flatley, the senior of the village, sat at the bar, nursing his one and only pint of the evening. He had seen more mischief than most and was regarded as the village's very own sage, albeit one with a penchant for colourful language and a love of traditional Irish dance.

Agnes leaned across the bar, all the time observing the conspiracy unfolding in the corner, "What do you think they're up to Michael? It's all looking very secretive"

Michael took a sip of his pint while he pondered his response. Replacing his glass carefully on the bar, he turned to Agnes, "Knowing those four, whatever it is, it'll be more fun as this village can handle."

And as he observed the quartet plotting their next escapade in hushed tones, Michael couldn't help but feel a twinge of nostalgia for his own days of youthful mischief. "Ah, to be young and foolish again," he mused, raising his glass in a silent toast to the boundless imagination of youth.

"Spudnik Weather Station," Finny declared, the first to throw out a smokescreen. "Aoife's got a grant to study atmospheric potato-growing conditions, and we're building a prototype launch… I mean, weather balloon."

Sheebie snorted. "Weather balloons don't need farmyard-sized launch pads, Finny."

"Ah, but this one does!" Finny countered, "It needs to be sturdy, able to withstand… uh… turbulent bog winds."

Aoife, rolling her eyes, chimed in, "And all these books are just about potato varieties for high-altitude cultivation. You know, the kind that sprout spuds as big as your head."

The villagers, ever gullible and ever-amused by the antics of their resident dreamers, chuckled and shook their heads. Biddy O'Rourke, however, wasn't convinced. Her face creased with suspicion as she observed the furtive glances and hushed conversations.

"There's somethin' more to all this. " she muttered, "What are you lot really up to?"

Their cover story, fragile as a cobweb in a gale, was unraveling. Finny, ever the optimist, tried to charm his way out of it, spinning a yarn about a potato-powered tractor race across the bog. Sheebie suggested they just ignore the whispers and focus on their project, but the watchful gaze of Biddy O'Rourke hung over them like a thundercloud.

They needed a new plan, something audacious enough to distract the village, something that wouldn't reveal their true intentions but would keep the rumour mill churning in a different direction. A plan bold, ridiculous, and quintessentially Ballymuckmore.

A mischievous grin spread across Finny's face as inspiration struck. "We're building a potato cannon," he declared, his voice ringing through the Pub. "The biggest, spud flinging contraption this side of Dublin Bay! We'll launch potatoes across the bog, rain down spuddy blessings on Widow O'Doyle's prize cabbages, and maybe even reach the edge of the county!"

The pub erupted in laughter. The villagers, always up for a bit of harmless mayhem, cheered the idea. Biddy O'Rourke, still suspicious but intrigued, grunted, "Spud cannons, eh? Well, see that they don't rain down on my prize-winning sheep, Finny McGillicuddy."

The Spudnik Rocket team had bought themselves some time, a smokescreen of potato projectiles and outlandish claims. They could work in the shadows, their real dream disguised by the absurdity of a spud-flinging cannon. The village would be watching for exploding potatoes, not celestial ambitions, and that was enough.

As the laughter subsided and the villagers dispersed, the friends exchanged knowing glances. They had pulled off the impossible – a cover story so ridiculous it was believable, so outlandish it wouldn't raise further suspicion.

Their quest for the stars, oiled by laughter, lunacy, and a healthy dose of potato-powered deception, had taken another turn. The dream of a rocket was still alive, cloaked in a haze of chaos, its true destination a secret whispered only amongst friends, beneath the vast, star-dusted sky of Ballymuckmore. The size of the rocket might still be up for debate, but one thing was certain: their space mission, born in the ashes of a moonshine-fuelled near-disaster, was on its way. And Ballymuckmore, a speck on the map with a universe in its heart, would soon be looking up, not just at the stars, but at their very own potato-powered rocket, streaking across the night sky, a tribute to the laughter, the lunacy, and the boundless, potcheen fermented dreams of a village on the edge of the bog.

Spud Fields and Stolen Smiles

Finny didn't remember the fire at his home, not truly. He recalled fragments – a searing orange glow against the night sky, the choking sting of smoke, the panicked shouts that morphed into a distant hum. He remembered the hospital, the sterile white walls and the hushed whispers of doctors, the dull ache in his limbs. But the fire itself, the heart of the tragedy that took his parents and his entire world, remained a blurry nightmare.

He woke up in Ballymuckmore, a small village nestled in the heart of Ireland, nestled amongst rolling green hills and endless fields of potatoes. His aunt and uncle, weathered and kind, took him in, their simple farmhouse his new haven. Finny adapted quickly, the wide-open spaces becoming his playground, the earthy scent of spuds his lullaby.

He was different, though. A shadow lingered in his eyes, a quietness that spoke of unspoken loss. But Finny, with his infectious grin and boundless energy, refused to be defined by his past. He found solace in laughter, in the company of his best friend, Sheebie, a fiery soul who could match him mischief for mischief. Together, they explored the world around them, building forts in the hay bales, racing across the fields with Seamus, the sheepdog, nipping at their heels, and dreaming of adventures beyond the spud fields.

Finny and Sheebie took a break from the madness that was beautifying Ballymuckmore, a chance to reflect and reminisce. Finny leaned against the hay bale, moonlight casting long shadows across the shed. Sheebie sat beside him, fiddling with a stray piece of straw, the resident mischievous glint in her eyes.

"Remember old Miss Higgins and her obsession with crochet?" Finny chuckled, the sound bouncing off the cluttered tools.
Sheebie snorted. "How could I forget? You 'accidentally' setting her prizewinning doily on fire during a 'spontaneous' science experiment."
Finny grinned, sheepishly rubbing the back of his neck. "Hey, I was testing the flammability of potato peels for the greater good of science!"
"Right, and the 'greater good' also involved turning the entire classroom into a smoke-filled disco with your 'potato disco ball,'" Sheebie added, her voice dripping with mock seriousness.
They both erupted in laughter, the memory vivid as if it happened yesterday. Their school days were a whirlwind of mischief, fired on by an insatiable curiosity and a shared disregard for authority. From rigging the school bell to play "Baa Baa Black Sheep" during the principal's speech to staging a potato-powered puppet show that ended in a mashed-potato-fuelled food fight, their escapades were legendary (and slightly terrifying for the teachers).
"Remember the time we convinced Seamus to herd the sheep through the schoolyard during lunch break?" Finny asked, wiping a tear of laughter from his eye.
Sheebie gasped, her eyes wide. "That was chaos! Principal O'Malley nearly fainted, convinced it was a sheep uprising led by a rogue shepherd."
"And who was that rogue shepherd ?" Finny winked, raising an eyebrow.
"Why, none other than the infamous Finbar McGillicuddy, of course!" Sheebie countered, throwing a playful punch at his arm.

The laughter subsided, replaced by a comfortable silence. The memories, though chaotic, were woven with a deep sense of camaraderie and shared adventure.

"We caused a lot of trouble, didn't we?" Finny said, a hint of nostalgia in his voice.

Sheebie nodded, a smile playing on her lips. "Enough to fill a whole field of spuds with stories. But wouldn't trade them for the world, would you?"

"Not a chance," Finny replied, his gaze meeting hers. "Those were the days, Sheebie. The days of potato-powered mayhem and boundless mischief."

But beneath the surface, the fire flickered in Finny. Sometimes, at night, when the moon cast long shadows across the fields, a pang of loneliness would pierce his heart. He yearned for memories he couldn't grasp as easily, for a past he couldn't reclaim. He'd stand by the window, gazing at the stars, whispering questions the wind carried away unanswered.

One day, while exploring his uncle's barn, Finny had stumbled upon a dusty trunk. Inside, nestled amongst moth-eaten scarves and faded photographs, lay a worn leather journal. It belonged to his mother, filled with her flowing script and colourful sketches. As he read, a forgotten world unfolded – vibrant city scapes, bustling markets, soaring cathedrals. He saw his parents, young and carefree, their smiles reflecting a life he never knew.

The journal became his treasure, a window to a past he desperately craved. He devoured the words, tracing his fingers over the faded drawings, piecing together the life that was stolen from him. He learned about their love for music, their passion for adventure, their dreams of traveling the world.

But with the knowledge came a bittersweet ache. He realised the life he had wasn't bad, but it wasn't his. He felt a

restlessness stirring within him, a yearning to break free from the spud fields and chase the whispers of his past, but Ballymuckmore was a safe haven, a shield against the nightmares that still, on occasion, visited him.
He had confided in Sheebie, her presence always a constant in his life, a grounding force that was never far away.

Unlikely Alliance

Finny's heart thumped a jig against his ribs as Constable O'Toole, a burly man with a handlebar moustache, pulled over a chair and planted himself at the end of their usual booth in the Pub with No Name.

His name was also Seamus, so to avoid any undue confusion between the sheepdog, the donkey and Finny's uncle, we'll just call him Constable O'Toole.

His eyes narrowed with suspicion, yet held a glint of mischief that didn't bode well for Finny's delicate secret.

"Word on the cobbles, McGillicuddy," the Constable boomed, voice thick with Galway brogue, "is that you're up to your usual shenanigans. Missing sheep shears, farm machinery and an alarming amount of hay disappearing from Farmer O'Malley's barn… any truth to these rumours?"

Finny swallowed hard, his throat suddenly as dry as the bog in summer. He glanced at Sheebie and Aoife, their faces masks of innocent confusion. But it was no use. Constable O'Toole knew him like the back of his hand, like the worn grooves of his beloved shillelagh.

"Would you believe it if I told you that sometimes the sheep like to shear themselves"

Constable O'Toole eyebrows already raised, went even higher. Dare Finny attempt to reveal the full capability of the Constable's eyebrows?

"Alright, Constable," Finny sighed, defeat hanging heavy in his voice. "We're not just building a potato cannon. We're building a Rocket. Spudnik. As in space, as in space rocket, as in…"

He trailed off, expecting the scoff, the arrest, the end of their dreams. But the Constable, instead of bursting into laughter as Finny had half-expected, just sat there, silent as a bog owl in the night. The seconds stretched, thick with awkward tension, until Finny feared his heart might burst from his chest like a ripe spud underfoot.

Finally, the Constable spoke, his voice surprisingly soft. "A rocket, you say? And powered by... potatoes?"

Sheebie snorted, but Aoife leaned forward, eyes gleaming with anticipation. Finny nodded, launching into a breathless explanation of their plans, the cobbled-together blueprints, the questionable fuel source, the audacious dream of Ballymuckmore leaving its mark on the cosmos.

Constable O'Toole listened, his face unreadable. And then, just as Finny expected the handcuffs to snap shut, the Constable did something unexpected. He threw his head back and laughed, a deep, belly-rumbling laugh that echoed through the pub.

When he finally caught his breath, tears streaming down his face, he wiped them with the back of his hand and shook his head. "Ah, McGillicuddy," he chuckled, "you never cease to amaze me. What harm can it do, eh? A bunch of dreamers with spuds and scrap metal trying to tickle the stars? Sounds like the kind of madness Ballymuckmore thrives on."

And just like that, Constable O'Toole, once a looming threat, became an unlikely ally. He offered his skills, his knowledge of the village's hidden nooks and crannies, his promise of turning a blind eye to the occasional "borrowing" of essential rocket parts.

He might not have believed in potato-powered flight, but he believed in Finny, Sheebie, and Aoife, in the unyielding spirit of Ballymuckmore and its boundless capacity for lunacy. Whether Leaky's infamous brew could propel a rocket to the stars, well, he'd seen stranger things after sampling his elixir, so anything was possible.

As the laughter faded and a new sense of purpose crackled in the air, one thing was clear: the Spudnik Rocket team had another member, one with a badge, a shillelagh, and a heart as big as the sky itself.

A mischievous glint sparkled in Constable O'Toole's eyes as he leaned against the bar of the Pub with No Name, relishing the ripple of gossip his announcement was about to cause. "Village tidy-up," he declared, puffing out his chest like a rooster ready to crow. "Official Garda order. All that rusting, hay-collecting junk littering the landscape has to go, or... well, let's just say Fergus might find himself with some company when you're mucking out the pound."

The villagers gasped, a collective shudder coursing through the pub. No one wanted to be within a hundred feet of O'Toole's mangy, flea-ridden mutt, Fergus. Grumbling and muttering, they promised clean-ups, swore to banish the rusty hulks from their fields.

To be fair to Constable O'Toole, at first he didn't want to be anywhere near Fergus either, but he had no choice, having 'inherited' him from a retiring officer in another village. However, Fergus may not be the brightest bulb in the box, but he had a heart of gold and in Ballymuckmore he fitted right in, being barking mad and all.

Over the next few days, true to his word, Constable O'Toole visited Leaky's shed in his Garda truck, its bed overflowing with reclaimed treasures. Rusted ploughs, weather-beaten harrows, even a dented milk churn winked in the sunlight. Leaky, ever the tinkerer, eyed the bounty with glee. "Now this is what I call inspiration, Constable! With a bit of elbow grease and moonshine-fuelled ingenuity, these could become..."

"Rocket parts, Leaky," Sheebie interjected, her voice firm. "Focus on the Spudnik, not your next contraption to scare the crows. Won't this stuff be missed ?"

The Constable chuckled, a low rumble that vibrated through his considerable moustache. "Don't worry, lass. Just a bit of creative borrowing for the greater good. Besides, if anyone asks, it's all part of the official village beautification project."

And so, under the watchful eye of the Constable and the amused whispers of the villagers, Leaky's shed transformed into a scrapyard wonderland. Cogs meshed with gears, rusty wheels found new purposes, and even the milk churn, with a few modifications, began to resemble a mini Spudnik.

Complaints from Farmer O'Malley about his missing hay baler were met with stern looks and muttered warnings about "Garda investigations."

Widow O'Doyle, on discovering the disappearance of her metal wind chime, simply shook her head and chuckled, muttering, "Those McGillicuddies, always up to something." The disappearance of the chime wasn't anything to do with the rocket, her neighbour saw the opportunity under the guise of the village cleanup, to get rid of the noisy, rusty eyesore.

Ballymuckmore, in its own chaotic way, became an accomplice in the Spudnik Rocket project. The village buzzed with whispered secrets, covert glances towards Leaky's shed, and a newfound appreciation for the transformative power of "official beautification projects."

The Constable, his badge a silent wink, proved to be an invaluable asset. He procured 'recycled' materials, deflected nosy questions, and even used his authority to clear a secluded field below the village, the perfect launchpad for their potato-powered dream.

A neglected crofter's cottage on the edge of the field made for an ideal Mission Control. Not only was it out of the wind and rain, but if would offer a level of protection should their interstellar machine encounter a rapid unscheduled disassembly when the historic moment of launch arrived. In other words, just in case it blows up.

The days following the Constables recruitment had been the most productive, with all manner of old equipment being 'relocated'. Leaky's barn was like a showcase for twentieth century farming in Ireland, the only thing missing was a full sized combine harvester, and that's only because they told Constable O'Toole that he had to take it back.

However, patience in the village was like Finny's favourite jumper, wearing a little thin. It all came to a head in the Pub. Constable O'Toole trying to enjoy a well deserved pint of Guinness, found himself boxed in.

The Constable, his chest puffed like a crowing rooster, surveyed the chaos that surrounded him. Villagers, cheeks flushed with righteous indignation, grumbled about missing wind chimes, mysteriously relocated tractors parts, and an alarming lack of hay in Farmer O'Malley's barn. The air crackled with suspicion, threatening to expose their Spudnik secret.

As quick as flash, O'Toole had a Eureka moment, the villagers needed something else to focus on. He slammed his mug on the counter, silencing the room. "Now listen here," he boomed, his voice thick with Ballymuckmore brogue. "We've cleared out all the eyesores cluttering the place, haven't we? Made it positively spud-sparkling! So why not put all this newfound beauty to good use? Enter the 'Beautiful Ireland' competition!"

The public bar fell silent, heads slowly swivelling towards the Constable. Then, like flowers turning to the sun, smiles bloomed across the faces of the Spudnik team. What a stroke of genius! A village spruced up, suspicions diverted, and a perfect cover for their rocket-building shenanigans.

Finny, his eyes sparkling with mischief, jumped up. "Brilliant, Constable O'Toole! We'll clean this place up like it's never been cleaned before. Flowers bursting everywhere, window boxes overflowing, even Seamus might get a bath!"

Which 'Seamus' in the village Finny was referring to was unclear, but they all nodded.

Aoife interjected, "Hold your horses, Finny. This needs organisation. Committees, subcommittees, brochures, catchy slogans…" Her eyes gleamed with the thrill of a new project, one that conveniently obscured their true objective.

Sheebie, always the voice of reason, chuckled. "Don't get too carried away, folks," she whispered. "Remember, the real prize is a rocket soaring above our heads, not a flowerpot trophy. Eyes on the prize"

But even she couldn't deny the appeal of the plan. A beautiful Ballymuckmore, basking in the spotlight of national competition, would be the perfect smokescreen for their space-bound ambitions. They could plant potatoes in hidden corners, disguise fuel tanks with prize-winning pumpkins, and launch their Spudnik Rocket under the cover of judging day fireworks.

With renewed fervour, the team set to work. Finny rallied the village in a whirlwind of flower-planting and window-box painting. Sheebie organised committees with names like "Petunia Posse" and "Blooming Bog Brigade." Aoife, armed with her trusty notebook, churned out brochure slogans like "Ballymuckmore: Sprouting Beauty, Reaching for Stardom."

The village buzzed with newfound purpose. Gardens were weeded, fences painted, even Seamus the donkey received a grudging scrub (though he remained unconvinced about the merits of floral headbands). As Ballymuckmore blossomed under the guise of beautification, their Spudnik Rocket, hidden in the heart of the chaos, started to take shape.

Leaky's shed, once a haven for dusty contraptions and near-death explosions, became a secret workshop. Hay balers transformed into launch modules, old milk churns morphed into fuel canisters, and the rhythmic clang of hammers masked the whispered calculations of celestial trajectories.

Constable O'Toole, meanwhile, played his part flawlessly. He shooed away nosy reporters, deflected suspicious questions with gruff pronouncements about 'official village beautification plans', and even managed to procure a few more 'borrowed' tools and materials that mysteriously found their way to Leaky's shed.

Ballymuckmore, in its own unique way, had become a united front. Under the banner of the Beautiful Ireland competition, villagers unknowingly charged a dream that stretched far beyond flowerbeds and prize pumpkins. For amidst the blooming petunias and freshly painted fences, a potato-powered dream was taking flight, a testament to the boundless lunacy and unwavering spirit of a village on the edge of the bog.

Galway Boy

Constable Seamus O'Toole had arrived in Ballymuckmore like a stray dog, tail between his legs and a shadow in his eyes. He hailed from the bustling city of Galway, a world away from the sleepy charm of the bog village. A bereavement, still raw and tender, had driven him to seek solace in the quiet countryside, hoping to drown his sorrows in the vastness of the sky and the whisper of the wind through the reeds.
Ballymuckmore was a shock to the system. The slow pace, the eccentric characters, the sheep outnumbering humans – it was a different reality altogether. Yet, amidst the strangeness, Seamus found a strange sense of peace. The villagers, with their open hearts and quirky humour, welcomed him with a warmth that surprised him. He found himself drawn to their stories, their dreams and their outlandish plans for the humble spud.
It was like stepping into a parallel universe where the only currency was laughter, and the only law was Murphy's Law. Being the Constable in Ballymuckmore wasn't exactly a high-pressure job. Most crimes involved sheep stuck in trees, misplaced dentures, and the occasional drunken brawl after a particularly spirited ceili. But Seamus took his role seriously, upholding the law with fairness and a twinkle in his eye. He learned to navigate the village's unwritten rules, the unspoken codes of conduct that kept the peace even better than any official statute.
He found himself drawn to Laoise, the golden haired angel who ran the post office. Her wit matched his, her laughter chased away the shadows that lingered in his soul. Their connection was undeniable, a slow burn that warmed him from

the inside out. But both were hesitant, carrying their own burdens and wary of opening their hearts.

Seamus, leaning against the Post Office counter, fiddled with his cap nervously. Laoise, sorting mail with practiced ease, sent him a teasing smile. "Are we out of stamps again, Constable?" Seamus blushed, feigning indignation. "Now would a fine Constable like myself be so ill prepared ? Merely admiring your exquisite collection, Miss Ahearn."

Laoise chuckled, her eyes twinkling. "So, what brings you to my humble abode this fine morning?"

Before Seamus could answer, the bell above the Post Office door jingled, announcing the arrival of Mrs. Flanagan, her basket overflowing with vegetables and gossip. He sighed, his hopeful smile fading.

"Just another stamp for Mrs. Flanagan then. Would you mind Constable?" Laoise asked, her smile equally strained.

"Aye, seems the whole village suddenly needs to send urgent letters," Seamus muttered, handing Mrs. Flanagan the stamp with a practiced smile.

As Mrs. Flanagan launched into a detailed account of her prize marrow's progress, Seamus stole a glance at Laoise. Her eyes sparkled with amusement, a silent understanding passing between them. This was their usual struggle: stolen moments for conversation amidst the constant stream of villagers needing stamps, parcels, and the occasional urgent need to borrow a cup of sugar.

The constant stream of customers continued: Mr. O'Sullivan needing a birthday card for his cat, Aoife sending a care package to her cousin in Dublin, Agnes dropping by for a chat and a gossip magazine. With each interruption, Seamus's hopeful expression would falter, only to be rekindled when Laoise caught his eye.

Finally, the door creaked shut. Silence descended, thick and unexpected.

Seamus and Laoise stared at each other, a hesitant smile blooming on both their faces. The moment stretched, filled with unspoken words and unspoken longing.

"So," Seamus began, his voice husky, "where were we?"

He leaned closer, his gaze meeting hers. Just then, the bell jangled again. They both jumped, startled, as young Mary burst in, breathless and excited.

"Laoise, guess what? My pet frog escaped! Can I put up a 'Lost Frog' poster?"

Seamus groaned, burying his face in his hands. Laoise, however, simply chuckled, her eyes twinkling.

"Of course you can, Mary," she said, ruffling the girl's hair. "But Seamus was just about to tell me a very interesting story…"

She cast Seamus a mischievous wink, and as they helped Mary with the poster, a different kind of warmth filled the Post Office, the warmth of shared laughter, unspoken affection, and the knowledge that their stolen moments, however brief, were all the sweeter for being shared in the heart of Ballymuckmore, amidst the chaos and the stamps.

Their secret romance had become an open secret, whispered over mugs of tea in Agnes's pub. The villagers, ever perceptive, saw the spark between them and smiled knowingly. They didn't need pronouncements or grand gestures; they understood the language of shared smiles, stolen glances, and lingering touches.

Time passed, and Ballymuckmore, with its gentle chaos and quirky charm, seeped into Seamus's bones. The village that had been a temporary refuge became his home, its people his family. He still carried the scars of his past, but they were softened by the laughter he shared with Finny, the wisdom he gleaned from Sheebie, and the warmth he found in Laoise's eyes.

Constable Seamus O'Toole, the city boy who came seeking solace, had found much more. He had found a community, a purpose, and a love that bloomed amidst the spuds and the sheep, a love as unique and enduring as the village itself. And as he walked hand-in-hand with Laoise, the setting sun painting the bog in hues of gold and orange, he knew he wouldn't trade his Ballymuckmore life, with all its quirks and eccentricities, for anything in the world.

Nuns on the Run

Finny tugged self-consciously at the itchy white wimple, feeling more like a spud with a sprout than a holy sister. He cast a disgruntled glance at Sheebie, who was humming merrily as she adjusted her own (admittedly more flattering) nun's habit.
"Sheebie, all due respect," Finny started, his voice strained, "but why, in the name of all that's holy, do I have to be a nun?"
Sheebie winked, her eyes sparkling with mischief. "Because, darling Finny, you have the most angelic face in Ballymuckmore. Even smothered in flour and soot, you radiate a certain… ethereal glow."
Finny snorted. "Ethereal? I look like a spud that fell into a milkmaid's laundry basket!"
"Nonsense! Besides," Sheebie continued, her voice dropping to a conspiratorial whisper, "think of the element of surprise. Imagine the good folk of St. Bartholomew's, expecting a pious sister, and getting you instead! It's comedic gold, Finny, pure gold!"
Finny groaned. "Comedic gold for you, maybe. I'm the one who'll be facing a mob of pitchfork wielding villagers if this goes south."
Sheebie patted his shoulder reassuringly. "Relax, love. I'll be scouting round to keep you safe, Leaky charming the locals with his, uh, theological expertise, and Seamus… well, Seamus will be Seamus. What could possibly go wrong?"
Finny raised an eyebrow skeptically. "Everything, that's what. But hey, at least if we get caught, I can claim temporary religious insanity brought on by too much spuddle-juice."
Sheebie burst out laughing, the sound echoing in the quiet barn. "Now that's an excuse even Father Dougal would struggle to

argue with! Come on, Finny, chin up! Think of it as an adventure, a potato-powered pilgrimage for the Spudnik cause!"

Finny sighed, knowing there was no point arguing with Sheebie once she had her mind set. He adjusted his wimple with a resigned shrug. "Alright, " he grumbled. "But if anyone asks, I identify as a spud-worshipping potato spirit trapped in a nun's habit. Just sayin'."

Sheebie grinned, throwing her arm around his shoulder. "Now that's the Finny I know! Now, let's go liberate that bell and launch Spudnik into history!"

And so, with a mix of trepidation and potato-fuelled determination, Finny, the reluctant nun, set off on his most unorthodox mission yet, leaving a trail of laughter and the faint scent of potcheen in his wake.

The hushed whispers of "Hail Mary, full of spuds" echoed through the moonlit churchyard, punctuated by the occasional muffled bark from Seamus, the sheepdog sporting a particularly fetching nun's habit two sizes too small. The Spudnik crew, their faces hidden under ill-fitting wimples, had embarked on a mission as holy as it was unorthodox: liberate the disused brass bell from St. Bartholomew's Church for their potato-powered rocket's engine nozzle.

Finny, channeling his inner Sister (with considerably less grace), led the charge, his hay cart disguised as a humble pilgrimage cart. Hay had been tied to the wheels of the cart, preventing any clattering as they crossed the old cobblestones. Aoife, ever the strategist, scouted the perimeter, her keen eyes searching for any sign of prying parishioners. Leaky, his pockets bulging with "holy" tools (read: spanners and screwdrivers) and moonlight bouncing off his beard, mumbled blessings under his breath, hoping they wouldn't attract unwanted celestial attention.

The bell tower of St. Bartholomew's loomed before them, a silent sentinel bathed in the pale moonlight. Finny, his wimple slightly askew, surveyed the scene with the air of a seasoned heist leader (which, admittedly, he wasn't). Aoife, perched on a nearby tombstone like a gargoyle come to life, scanned the perimeter for any sign of wakeful parishioners. Leaky fidgeted nervously, muttering a garbled prayer under his breath.

Their plan was audacious, bordering on heroic. Using ropes fashioned from bedsheets "borrowed" from Agnes's washing line, they would scale the walls of the belfry tower, climb in through the window, liberate the bell and lower it down to the cart waiting below. What could possibly go wrong?

With a mighty heave, Finny, also the muscle of the operation, launched the grappling iron towards the window some twenty feet above. The iron soared through the air like a determined acrobat, its target seemingly beckoning it closer. But alas, it clattered to the ground in front of him, eliciting a collective "Shhh!" from his comrades.

"Five feet? Is that all you can manage?" Aoife whispered incredulously, her disappointment palpable.

"I just need a bit of practice, that's all," Finny muttered, sheepish in the face of failure as he retrieved the rope.

Meanwhile, Leaky tip-toed over to the tower and cautiously turned the handle on the door, which emitted a loud creak as it swung open. "Shall we take the stairs?" he suggested, attempting to salvage the situation.

It was, without a doubt, not the auspicious start they had hoped for.

Leaky leading the way with surprising agility (perhaps energised by the pre-heist potcheen he'd stashed in his habit).

Reaching the belfry, they found the bell shrouded in dust sheets, its bronze form gleaming faintly in the moonbeams. Sheebie's job was to keep a look out for any villagers that might have ideas on scuppering the current acquisition.
Their first hurdle was to silence the clapper. One touch on the rim of the bell, their presence would be alerted to the slumbering village and the game would be up.
Removing the clapper, however, proved more challenging than anticipated. As the bell was slowly hoisted into the air, the ropes groaning under its weight, threatening to snap and send the bell, and them, through the rickety wooden belfry floor.
Leaky produced his "holy tools" with a flourish and disappeared under the rim of the bell only to reappear a moment later. "Wrong size. It doesn't fit"
"What do you mean wrong size?" Finny hissed, straining as he held the entire weight of the bell.
"There must be tools around here somewhere" Leaky set about searching the belfry for something, anything to help remove the clapper.
"Anytime would be good Leaky".The sweat beading on Finny's forehead.
It seemed that good fortune had smiled on them, as there, in the corner by the wooden slatted window, was a toolbox containing just the right 'holy' tool.
The clapper, thankfully, proved easier to detach than a stubborn barnacle and Finny gently lowered the bell back to its resting place and took a breath.
Aoife crouched by the lip of the hay cart, moonlight glinting off her determined eyes. The bell, an imposing bronze disc shrouded in dust sheets, sat precariously on the edge of the window above her, threatening to topple at the slightest misstep. Finny and Leaky, faces grimy and breaths heavy,

stood on either side of the bell, ropes straining in their calloused hands.

"Alright, lads," Aoife whispered, her voice tight with tension, "remember, smooth and steady. This ain't a spud sack race, we need finesse."

Finny grunted, his brow furrowed in concentration. "Easy for you to say, you ain't the one with rope burn diggin' into your palms!"

Aoife shot him a playful jab. "Quit your whinging, Finny. Think of it as training for your spud-lifting championship dreams."

Leaky chuckled, though the sound was strained. "Aye, at least then we'd be lifting spuds, not a church bell that weighs more than Agnes's prize pumpkin."

Ignoring their banter, Aoife focused on the task at hand. "Alright, on my mark. One, two..." she counted, her voice low and controlled. "Three!"

With a synchronised grunt, Finny and Leaky lowered the bell inch by painful inch. The ropes groaned, the hay creaked, and Seamus, ever the enthusiastic observer, let out a curious bark.

"Careful with Seamus, Leaky!" Aoife hissed. "We don't need him attracting any unwanted attention."

"Sorry, Aoife," Leaky mumbled, trying to soothe the excited sheepdog with a quick scratch behind the ears whilst holding half the weight.

The bell lowered further, its bronze form partially visible beneath the dust sheet. Aoife held her breath.

"Almost there," she whispered, her voice barely audible. "Just a bit more, steady..."

With a final heave, the bell landed with a soft thud on the bed of hay. Relief washed over them, as palpable as the scent of damp earth and potcheen fumes.

"See, that wasn't so bad," Aoife said, a triumphant grin spreading across her face. "Now, let's get this chariot outta here before the whole village decides to join our 'pilgrimage.'"
Finny and Leaky, their muscles protesting, managed weak smiles. They knew their escape was far from over, but for now, they had their prize. The bell, the heart of their Spudnik, was theirs.
Triumphant whispers filled the air, quickly dissolving into panicked hisses as lights flickered on in nearby houses, and the sound of approaching footsteps sent shivers down their spines. The footsteps were Sheebie's "Time to go ladies "
Thinking fast, Aoife covered the bell with a potato sack they'd brought for "religious" purposes (Leaky's quick thinking, powered by another swig of potcheen).
Leaky threw the grappling iron into the cart below, next to the bell and followed Finny who was already making his escape down the stairs, his wimple now completely askew, followed close behind, Seamus nipping excitedly at his heels.
Seamus, emboldened by the chaos, let out a triumphant bark, alerting the entire village to their presence. As they scrambled to their feet, the cry of "Who goes there?" echoed through the night, and the Spudnik crew's Operation Holy Roller took a hilarious, and potentially disastrous, turn.
With the bell secured (precariously, it must be said) on the hay cart, the Spudnik crew knew their visit to St. Bartholomew's churchyard was at an end. The panicked shouts of "Who goes there?" were growing closer, homing in on the unholy racket Seamus was raising with his excited barks.
Finny, ever the resourceful leader (though his wimple was now hanging by a thread), whipped the makeshift "pilgrimage chariot" into action. Leaky, his face now a comical mix of soot and determination, pushed from behind with Sheebie, his "holy

tools" clattering like misplaced altar bells. Seamus, oblivious to the danger, bounced happily beside them, his sheepdog instincts temporarily overwhelmed by the thrill of the chase. Their escape route was a winding path through the graveyard, littered with headstones and the occasional startled owl. The hay cart, laden with the hefty bell, creaked and groaned like a haunted carriage. Aoife, perched on the back like a mischievous gargoyle, one hand on their treasure, scanned their pursuers, barking instructions.

The night air was thick with the scent of damp earth and adrenaline. Flashlights danced in the darkness, casting grotesque shadows on the headstones. The villagers, armed with pitchforks and righteous indignation, were gaining ground.

The hay on the wheels had served its purpose on their approach, but now as the cart clattered over the cobblestones through the graveyard, one of the metal rims threw a spark. Before long both wheels were ablaze.

The sight was one to see. Four ghostly Nuns running with a fiery cart through the graveyard. A hell hound at their feet. It was enough for even the most non religious villagers, and there was only two in that village, to cross themselves and pray for divine intervention.

That came in the form of Seamus O'Malley (no relation to the sheepdog) as he blocked their path, brandishing a pitchfork the size of a small tree.

"Hold, heathens!" he bellowed, his voice laced with suspicion. "What unholy cargo do you carry?"

Finny, fixing his wimple and ever the quick thinker (aided by a generous dollop of potcheen courage), threw himself into a dramatic bow. "Forgive us, good sir! We are but humble nuns, returning from a sacred quest!" His soft Killarney accent was very convincing.

"Sacred quest, eh?" O'Malley eyed them skeptically. "And what might this 'sacred quest' be?"

Aoife, ever the diplomat, stepped forward. "We've been blessed with a vision," she declared, her voice ringing with conviction. "A vision of a glorious harvest, brought forth by the power of the ancient relic of St Spudius!"

She gestured dramatically at the bell, now shrouded in a potato sack to hide its true nature. "And this, good sir, is the key to unlocking that bounty! We must deliver it to the Whispering Bog before dawn!"

The four nuns stood in silent prayer as O'Malley surveyed the situation.

Sister Leaky nervously stroked his beard.

O'Malley, a man of simple faith and even simpler logic, scratched his head in bewilderment. "The Whispering Bog at dawn, St Spudius you say? Hmmm... the spuds are indeed ailing this year. Perhaps there's something to your tale..."

He lowered his pitchfork, albeit cautiously. "Very well. Continue on your 'sacred quest' sisters, but be warned, any further mischief and you'll answer to me!"

With a relieved nod, the Spudnik crew whipped the cart into motion, Seamus leading the charge with renewed enthusiasm. The villagers watched them go, their initial anger replaced by a mixture of curiosity and confusion.

As they sped away, the adrenaline slowly subsided, replaced by the weight of their near miss and the absurdity of their situation. They didn't look particularly holy, their wimples askew, their faces streaked with mud and moonlight, but they had their prize.

They had escaped, but their journey was far from over. The road ahead was fraught with danger and potential hilarity. But one thing was certain: the Spudnik crew, with their unorthodox methods and unwavering determination, were just getting started on their potato-powered adventure.

Back in Ballymuckmore, midst gales of laughter and relieved sighs, they surveyed the damage. The bell was slightly dented, but nothing that a few good whacks with a hammer couldn't cure, and the village was already buzzing with the tale of the "Nuns and their Fiery Chariot who Stole the Bell from St Bartholomew's "

As Aoife tinkered with the bell, a glint in her eye, Finny couldn't help but grin. "Well," he chuckled, "that wasn't exactly Operation Holy Roller, was it?"

Aoife winked. "Not exactly," she admitted, "but hey, at least Spudnik has an engine nozzle, and we gained a legendary story for the pub."

And so, the Spudnik crew, a little worse for wear but their spirits soaring, continued their quest to launch their potato-powered rocket. Their journey may have begun with a slightly unorthodox "borrowing," but it was a testament to their ingenuity, their unwavering friendship, and their ability to find humour even in the most harebrained of situations. After all, who needs a conventional rocket launch when you have a band of potato-loving lunatics, a bunch of nun's habits and a whole lot of distilled spirit?

Bonanza is reborn

Finny's eyes widened like miniature moons upon hearing the news. Farmer O'Malley, notorious for his grumpy disposition and suspiciously well-guarded hay supply, was tearing down the old grain silo! It felt like destiny knocking, not with its bony knuckles, but with a rusty silo door creaking open.
"The answer to our size problem, Sheebie!" he exclaimed, his voice trembling with excitement. "That silo, it's practically begging for a Spudnik Rocket!"
Sheebie, ever the voice of reason, raised an eyebrow. "Finny, a silo? Are you sure? That thing's about as aerodynamic as a brick in a bathtub."
But Finny, spurred on by a potent mix of moonshine and inspiration, wouldn't be deterred. He enlisted the help of Constable O'Toole, whose charm offensive (a gruff smile and promises of borrowed equipment) managed to melt even Farmer O'Malley's gruff exterior. With much creaking, groaning, and strategically placed pints of Guinness, the silo was transported piece by piece to the launchpad, looking every bit like a disused giant pepper pot on a field trip.
Constable O'Toole suggested a competition to provide a name for the new focus of the village's Beautiful Ireland entry, while its surface, a canvas for youthful dreams, would blossom under the touch of five little paintbrushes, guided by the whimsical vision of Mrs. O'Flaherty, their teacher.
Posters adorned lampposts, handwritten flyers fluttered under doors, and the announcement echoed through the village square like a spirited ceili call. Young and old, farmers and dreamers, everyone was invited to submit their entry, their chance to etch their name in Ballymuckmore's history.

Entries poured in, as diverse as the village itself. Aoife, with her fiery spirit, favoured "Big Bogland Bonanza Beacon." Sheebie, ever practical, suggested "The Emerald Granary," a name grounded in purpose. Agnes, with a twinkle in her eye, submitted "Seamus's Secret Stash," much to the amusement (and slight annoyance) of the Constable. Leaky suggested keeping with village tradition and calling it the "Silo with No Name".

Laughter filled the air as villagers debated the merits of each entry. Mrs. O'Flaherty, convinced the silo resembled a giant spud, championed "The Mighty Murph," while Mickey the Milkman, inspired by its new coat of paint, argued for "The Emerald Spire."

Whilst entries continued to mount up, the design for the exterior was nearing completion. Seamus, the sheepdog had been transformed into a shepherd, herded sheep across a twilight sky. A leprechaun, sporting a jaunty potato-green hat, piloted a rocket shaped like a giant baked potato, exhaust flames a fiery swirl of ketchup and mustard. Widow O'Doyle's prize-winning cabbage, inexplicably sprouting wings, soared alongside a grinning Finny, astride a moonbeam.

Sheebie and Aoife, armed with paintbrushes and buckets of laughter, began the translation of this fantastical dream onto the Bonanza's steel skin. Sheebie, her movements precise and sure, brought Seamus's watchful eyes to life, each stroke imbued with the quiet poetry of the night sky. Aoife, her brushstrokes imparted a frenetic energy, captured the leprechaun's mischievous grin and the potato rocket's comical trajectory.

The Bonanza became a living storybook, a testament to Ballymuckmore's unbridled imagination. Tourists, lured by the Beautiful Ireland competition, gasped at the whimsical murals, marvelling at the village's artistic charm. Little did they know, beneath the playful potato astronauts and flying cabbages, a real rocket dreamt of the stars.

Sheebie, unable to contain her excitement, would sneak around the Bonanza, tracing the painted dreams with her fingers. Seamus, his tail wagging in approval, would follow, nose brushing against the imaginatively shaped constellations. Even Constable O'Toole, his gruff exterior masking a secret smile, would pause on his rounds, admiring the leprechaun's cheeky wink.

The painting transformed the Bonanza from a mere disguise into a celebration, a shared canvas for Ballymuckmore's hopes and dreams. It wasn't just a rocket anymore; it was a vessel carrying not just potatoes and scrap metal, but the laughter of children, the pride of a village, and the boundless lunacy that dared to reach for the stars.

The naming day had arrived and the village was a hive of anticipation. Agnes, Seamus, Leaky, Aoife, and Finny, a motley crew united by their love for Ballymuckmore, donned their most serious expressions (well, as serious as they could manage) and pored over the entries. Laughter mingled with thoughtful murmurs as they weighed each name, its meaning, its connection to the village, its ability to sing on the tongue. Finally, after much deliberation and good-natured bickering, they had a shortlist. They folded each remaining suggestion into identical slips of paper, placed them in a battered straw hat that had seen countless ceili dances, and with bated breath, Constable O'Toole drew the winning entry.

He unfolded the paper, a hush falling over the gathered crowd. "And the new name for our magnificent grain silo," he declared, a grin spreading across his face, "is… Grainy McGrain Face"

There was a collective gasp from the assembled villagers.

"Just kidding." The Constable smile, "The real name is …
Ballymuckmore Bonanza"

Cheers erupted, echoing through the village square. The name resonated, capturing the essence of Ballymuckmore – its verdant landscape, its agricultural heart, and the spirit of community that bloomed within it.

The chosen name was emblazoned across its side in bold, emerald letters. It stood tall, a beacon of beauty and pride, a testament to the village's creativity and their unwavering belief in the magic of a good name, a shared dream, and a community that thrived on laughter, spuds, and the occasional potcheen-fuelled adventure.

As the final brushstroke landed on the leprechaun's potato rocket, a hush fell over the gathering crowd. Mrs. O'Flaherty, beaming like a proud sun, clapped her hands. "There, my darlings," she declared. "Ballymuckmore's own masterpiece, ready to take on the world!"

The village erupted in cheers, unaware of the embryonic rocket hidden within the Bonanza's belly. But Finny, Sheebie, Aoife, and Leaky knew. This wasn't just a competition; it was a launchpad, a stage for their orbital dream, now adorned with the laughter and art of their village. The Bonanza, a testament to Ballymuckmore's lunacy and its love for everything out of the ordinary, stood poised to rewrite the script, not just of the Beautiful Ireland competition, but of Ballymuckmore's place in the cosmos.

HQ for the Beautiful Ireland competition was only ever going to be the Pub with No Name. If help was ever needed, it could always be found in the Pub, although the usefulness of the help was inversely proportional to the hours the Pub had been open.

It was the go-to spot for celebrations in the village, although to be fair, the options were as limited as a sheep's vocabulary - maybe the Post Office, if you were feeling wild.
But when it came to marking achievements, the Pub with No Name took the biscuit, or the spud pie, and there was none more grand than Bonanza.
Agnes, pouring drinks faster than a politician dodging questions, could barely keep up with the demands of her thirsty patrons. Sean, attempting to play the role of culinary hero by ferrying snacks from the kitchen, found that by the time he reached the long table Agnes had cleared, his tray resembled a prop from a magician's act – empty, with no trace of the goodies that once adorned it.
The Spudnik crew nestled into their customary booth, savouring every frothy sip of their pints of Guinness like it was the elixir of life. Sheebie was deep in thought, her brow furrowed between sips
"So, let me get this straight," she said, her voice thick with porridge oats and confusion. "We've got Farmer O'Malley's grain silo, taller than a Pooka on stilts, and we're… gonna strap an engine to it? I get the potato power and all, but how in the bog's name is that supposed to take flight?"
Finny, his cheeks puffed with a potato pancake, grinned at her bewilderment. "Ah, Sheebie," he explained, his voice dripping with the honeyed tones of Ballymuckmore's resident dreamer, "that's where you're missing the big spud in the bucket. Bonanza isn't going anywhere. We're building Spudnik inside Bonanza!"
Aoife, her eyes sparkling with the light of celestial equations, chimed in. "Think of it as a potato-powered Trojan horse," she said, a playful glint in her eyes. "The big old silo becomes our launch pad, disguised as a rustic grain storage facility. Once

Spudnik's ready, we unleash the beast from its belly, and away it goes!"

Sheebie's mind reeled, trying to visualise this potato-powered contraption emerging from the belly of a grain silo. It was as clear as mud, yet somehow, with Finny's infectious enthusiasm and Aoife's scientific assurance, it made a twisted kind of sense.

"And the doors?" Sheebie questioned, remembering the cavernous openings on either side of Bonanza.

Finny patted the table with a flourish. "Ah, yes, the secret ingredient! We've reinforced the hinges and fitted them with powered winches. Come launch day, those doors will swing open like the gates of potato heaven, revealing Spudnik, well the bottom of Spudnik, in all its glorious, metallic majesty!"

Aoife chuckled, adding, "And the top of the silo? We've rigged it to detach seamlessly, creating a grand escape hatch for our Spudnik rocket."

Sheebie stared at them, her mouth agape, a single potato chip dangling precariously from her finger. In her mind, Spudnik danced a jig inside the silo, its potato flames erupting from the open hatch, a spectacle as lunacy-fuelled as anything Ballymuckmore had ever witnessed.

Seamus twitched his ears, he found the whole idea fanciful, but thought best not to say anything , as usual. And anyway, what was a donkey doing stood at the bar ?

The plan, while still as clear as mud to anyone outside these potcheen addled minds, held a spark of outrageous brilliance. It was a testament to Ballymuckmore's spirit, a cosmic cocktail of lunacy and dreams. And as they continued their drinks, one thing was certain: Spudnik, nestled within the belly of Bonanza, would be ready to take flight, potato by glorious potato, into the vast unknown of the Irish sky.

Wool and Wanderlust

Sheebie wasn't born with a silver spoon, but she was born with a silver whistle. Its tarnished gleam and worn mouthpiece held the key to her kingdom – the rolling hills and emerald pastures of Ballymuckmore. From the moment she could walk, she was shepherding, her whistle cutting through the air, a melody she understood better than any human tongue.
Her world was measured in bleats and wool, sunrises painting the sky gold and sunsets igniting it with orange fire. The rhythm of the seasons dictated her life - lambing in spring, the shearers' laughter in summer, the comforting weight of fleece against her skin in winter. School was a necessary but unwelcome distraction, its walls confining compared to the endless expanse of sky above the hills.
Sheebie was no dunce, mind you. The village schoolmaster often spoke of her "above average intelligence," but book smarts felt hollow compared to the wisdom gleaned from watching a ewe care for her newborn or coaxing a stubborn ram back to the fold. Her lessons were written in the clouds, whispered by the wind, and etched in the patterns of sheep tracks across the dew-kissed grass.
Her parents, weathered and practical, saw a future for their daughter beyond the sheepfold. They dreamt of her as a doctor in Dublin, a teacher in Cork, her sharp mind blossoming in a world far wider than Ballymuckmore. But Sheebie felt a pang of disquiet at the thought. The city's clamour sounded harsh compared to the wind whistling through the heather, the cobblestones cold against her wool-booted feet.
Still, she didn't resist their wishes completely. She ventured into the towns for the annual festival, the bright lights and bustling crowds both exhilarating and overwhelming. She even

spent a month with her aunt in Dublin, experiencing the cacophony of city life. Yet, each time, she returned to Ballymuckmore with a renewed appreciation for its quietude, the familiar scent of sheep wool grounding her like a comforting blanket.

Sheebie perched on a moss-covered rock, the midday sun warming her back as she watched her flock graze peacefully. Seamus, her loyal sheepdog, lay beside her, his head resting on her outstretched leg. She sighed, a wistful note in her voice.

"Seamus," she began, stroking his fur absentmindedly, "do you ever wonder what's beyond these hills? Do you think there's more to life than chasing sheep and watching the seasons turn?"

Seamus pricked his ears, his gaze flicking towards the distant horizon. A low whine escaped his throat, almost questioning.

"Da says I should be a doctor in Dublin," she continued, her voice tinged with bitterness. "Aunt Moira wanted me to stay with her, learn about city life. They think I'm wasting my mind here, Seamus."

Seamus nudged her hand with his wet nose, a silent plea to stay focused on the present.

"But sometimes," Sheebie confessed, her voice dropping to a whisper, "I feel like there's a whole world out there waiting for me. Places I haven't seen, people I haven't met, things I haven't learned."

Seamus let out a soft bark, his tail thumping a slow rhythm against the ground. It wasn't a bark of excitement, but one of understanding, a silent acknowledgment of her yearning.

"But then I look at you," she said, scratching behind his ears, "and I see contentment. You don't chase city lights, Seamus. You find joy in the simple things – a good belly rub, a well-herded flock, a nap in the sun."

Seamus rolled onto his back, offering his belly for a rub, a playful glint in his eyes. It was his way of saying, "Happiness isn't about where you are, Sheebie, but who you're with." Sheebie laughed, the sound echoing across the hills. "You're right, old friend," she said, burying her face in his fur. "Maybe I don't need to leave Ballymuckmore to find my purpose. Maybe it's right here, woven into the wool and the wind and the bleats of my sheep."

Seamus let out a contented sigh, his tail thumping a faster rhythm now, a silent agreement. They sat in comfortable silence for a while, Sheebie's worries dissipating like mist under the warm sun. Perhaps her future wasn't a choice between city lights and sheepfolds, but a tapestry woven with both, as vibrant and unique as the rolling hills of Ballymuckmore and the loyal sheepdog by her side.

As the sun began its descent, painting the sky in hues of orange and pink, Sheebie rose, her heart lighter. Seamus trotted beside her, his presence a constant reminder that sometimes, the greatest adventures are found not in the distance, but in the depth of connection with the world around you, and the furry friend who walks by your side.

Sheebie, the girl of the hills, might never leave Ballymuckmore entirely, but her heart, like the clouds above, would forever dance between the familiar and the faraway, her life a tapestry woven with wool and wanderlust, as unique and vibrant as the land she called home.

Ten Paces

The late afternoon sun cast long shadows across the farmyard, painting elongated stripes across the side of Farmer Brennan's barn. The air hung heavy with the scent of drying hay and the distant bleating of sheep. Farmer Brennan, however, was oblivious to the pastoral peace. His brow furrowed deeper than a potato forgotten in the field, his boots pounding a restless rhythm against the dusty ground.
He marched determinedly along the side of the barn, counting under his breath. 1, 2, 3… 28, 29… Thirty steps.
Mary, his wife, watched from the porch, a knowing smile playing on her lips. Her hands, rough but kind, rested on her ample hips. "Brennan, love," she drawled, her voice as warm and comforting as a mug of potcheen on a cold day, "what's got you stomping about like a rooster with sore feet?"
"Quiet woman. Can you not see I'm busy." Farmer Brennan retorted angrily, "Now I've got to start over." He turned and marched purposefully back to the end of the barn and started again, his count echoing through the quiet farmyard. 1, 2, 3… 27, 28, 29… Thirty steps."
Brennan stopped, his chest heaving like a bellows. He pointed a crooked finger at the barn. "Mary, see this? See it, woman? It's shrunk! Thirty feet shorter, it is! Yesterday, it reached clear to that oak tree, now look at it!"
Mary followed his gaze, her smile widening. The barn stood as it always had, solid and unyielding. "Now, Brennan," she chuckled, her voice tinged with gentle amusement, "you've been working yourself too hard, it's bound to play tricks on your mind. Come now, sit a spell, have a cup of tea, and you'll see it's all in your head."

Brennan grumbled, but the familiar warmth of her voice and the promise of tea soothed his ruffled feathers. He settled onto the porch with a sigh, accepting the steaming mug from Mary's hand. As he sipped, her words began to settle in. He had been pushing himself. Maybe Mary was right. Maybe the barn hadn't shrunk. Maybe it was just his imagination, stretched thin by too much potcheen and not enough sleep.

She patted his arm gently. "Come on then, love," she said, her voice warm. "I got some leftover spud pie that'll set you right. Sleep it off, and by mornin', that barn will be back to its usual self, I'm sure."

Brennan nodded, a flicker of hope rekindled in his eyes. As he watched the last rays of sunlight paint the sky in hues of orange and purple, he couldn't help but smile. Mary was right. It was probably just the exhaustion playing tricks on him. After a good night's sleep, the barn would be back to its normal size, and he'd be back to his usual self

Meanwhile, Bonanza buzzed with the frenetic energy of dreams taking shape. In the heart of the village, Leaky, Finny, Aoife, and Sheebie were locked in a dance of construction, transforming thirty feet of a once-proud barn into the launch gantry for Spudnik.

Leaky, his beard bristling with excitement, orchestrated the chaos like a conductor leading an unorthodox symphony. He pointed, shouted instructions, and occasionally muttered to himself about the "celestial mechanics of spud propulsion" while adjusting his ever-present goggles.

Finny, the picture of grease-stained determination, wrestled with metal beams twice his size. He grunted, he cursed (under his breath, mind you), but he never faltered, driven by the thought of Spudnik soaring through the cosmos.

The barn, once a sturdy shelter for Farmer Brennan's sheep and hay, was now undergoing a spectacular metamorphosis. Its metal frame, liberated with the "generous assistance" of a few borrowed tools and a touch of Ballymuckmore ingenuity, were being transformed into the skeleton of Spudnik's launch gantry. Finny, wiping the sweat from his brow with a grease-stained sleeve, grinned at Sheebie. "Alright, Sheebie," he conceded, his voice hoarse from shouting instructions, "I gotta admit, you were a spud-tastic genius with that 'borrowed' barn idea."
Sheebie raised an eyebrow but a smile tugged at her lips. "Desperate times call for... unorthodox solutions, Finny. Besides, Farmer Brennan probably spends more time napping in the shade than measuring his barn these days."
Aoife, perched atop a precarious pile of metal scraps, chimed in. "And let's face it, thirty feet is a significant chunk of barn. Even Brennan's legendary obliviousness has its limits."
Leaky, adjusting his goggles while muttering about the "spudcentric gravitational pull" of the gantry, looked up with a knowing glint in his eye. "Besides, we gave it back! Bolted those end panels right on, good as new. Just... slightly shorter."
The thirty-foot structure, welded and bolted together with a healthy dose of determination and a sprinkle of potcheen-induced inspiration, was slowly rising towards the sky. It wasn't perfect, mind you. The welds might have been a bit more artistic than structurally sound, and the overall design owed more to sheer enthusiasm than textbook engineering. But it was theirs, a testament to the village's spirit, held together by the invisible threads of friendship, lunacy, and an unshakeable belief that even the most audacious dreams could take flight, potato-powered or not.
Leaky, armed with his trusty toolbox and a lifetime of tinkering experience, continued to work his magic. The silo's rusty

interior was a hive of activity. Pipes were repurposed for fuel lines, and a control panel cobbled together from salvaged tractor parts winked promisingly in the dim light.

Aoife, her fiery hair escaping its braid in a halo of energy, split her time between plotted trajectories and keeping everyone hydrated with generous swigs from a mysterious flask labeled "Rocket Fuel" (which, Sheebie suspected, contained more tea than actual fuel).

While Sheebie, armed with a tape measure and a steely glint in her eye, ensured every modification adhered to the "official Ballymuckmore Bonanza blueprint," a document carefully crafted to both disguise the rocket and win the competition. Under the cloak of blooming, the Spudnik Rocket, disguised as a whimsical celebration of rural Ireland, began to take shape. Each clang of a hammer, each whispered calculation, each sheep shaped mural painted on the exterior, became a brick in the foundation of their space-bound dream.

Sheebie, ever the voice of reason, kept a watchful eye on the proceedings. She double-checked measurements, ensured safety protocols were followed, and occasionally reminded the others that dreams were all well and good, but they still needed their eyebrows intact for the post-launch celebrations.

As the sun dipped below the horizon, casting long shadows across the bog, the gantry stood tall within Bonanza which stood as a silhouette against the twilight sky. The team, exhausted but exhilarated, gathered around, their faces lit by the dying light and the shared glow of their accomplishment. They had taken thirty feet of barn and turned it into a launchpad for the impossible. And as they looked at their handiwork, they knew, with a certainty that transcended logic, that Spudnik, the potato-propelled dream, was one step closer to becoming a reality.

Zorg

Aoife's face crumpled, mirroring the deflated dreams of the Spudnik crew. The pub, usually abuzz with their boisterous plans, was heavy with the silence of a fallen star. She had tested every combination, from raw potcheen to triple-distilled moonshine, but the meagre flames produced barely managed to singe a hay bale, let alone propel a rocket into the abyss.
"It's no use," Aoife choked out, her voice thick with tears and potato fumes. "Spudnik's grounded. We can't fly on dreams and fumes."
Finny's grin, usually as constant as the moon, flickered, then vanished. Sheebie slumped on her elbows, eyes dull with disappointment. Even Leaky, his tinkering spirit usually irrepressible, stared dejectedly into his mug.
Suddenly, a gruff voice broke the mournful silence. "I might have a spud in the right barrel for ye."
From the shadowed corner next to their usual booth, a figure emerged, his face shrouded by a wide-brimmed hat. The air crackled with anticipation, whispers flitting across the room like bats in the twilight. Leaky, eyes wide with excitement, gasped, "By the peat fires of Ballymuckmore! Zorg!"
Legends swirled around Zorg, a shadowy figure said to possess the secrets of the most potent potcheen this side of the Milky Way. His brews, whispered of in hushed tones, were said to fuel leprechaun mischief and power rickety jalopies across the bog at the speed of lightning.
The crew watched, hearts pounding like sheepskin drums, as Zorg slowly removed his hat. His face, weathered like an old leather boot, creased into a knowing smile. "Heard a rumour you young'uns were brewing something. Aiming for the stars

are ye," he drawled, his voice as smooth as aged whiskey. "But without the right fuel, you'll be stuck in the bog forever."
He reached into his cloak, retrieving a clay jug, its surface swirling with mysterious runes. A heavy aroma, pungent and intoxicating, filled the air, making Finny's eyes water and Seamus bark with excitement. This wasn't your Grandpa O'Malley's moonshine; this was liquid rocket fuel, bottled magic from the heart of the bog.
Zorg uncorked the jug, and a wisp of purple smoke curled upwards, shimmering like a captured nebula. "This, me darling's," he declared, "is 'Zorg's Zenith', the elixir that'll send your Spudnik to the moon and back. it'll light up the sky all the way to the Shannon and beyond."
Hope, like a spark from a flint, ignited in the eyes of the Spudnik crew. Finny's grin returned, as bright as a full moon. Sheebie sat up straight, her pragmatism momentarily forgotten. Even Leaky's gears seemed to whir to life, lubricated by the potent scent of Zorg's magic brew.
With Zorg's Zenith as their new moonbeam, the Spudnik team had been thrown a lifeline. The dream of Ballymuckmore reaching for the stars wasn't dead; it was simply waiting for the right fuel, the right spark, the right legend to give it the shove it needed.
The pub, once shrouded in the melancholic haze of deflated dreams, now buzzed with renewed energy. Zorg, the shrouded alchemist, became their unlikely saviour, weaving his potato-powered magic into the heart of Spudnik. With his potent fuel and Leaky's ingenious modifications, the rocket, once an empty promise, began to hum with the anticipation of flight.
A cautious smile played on Aoife's lips as she eyed Zorg's clay jug, a flicker of doubt battling with the thrill of hope in her eyes. "Alright, Zorg," she said, her voice firm yet laced with a

hint of respect, "we're not about to launch Spudnik on a whim. We need to see your Zenith strut its stuff."
"Well, there's no time like the present. Have you got something to test it in ?" The excitement clearly visible in Zorg's eyes.
"Er, probably best to leave it 'til the morning." Sheebie suggested. "Lots of curtain twitchers about"
The bog, shrouded in the ethereal mist of predawn, was their testing ground, away from prying eyes. To test their potcheen rocket fuel, Aoife had built a miniature Spudnik. A scaled-down version of their space-bound dream, cobbled together from a dented milk churn with rudimentary engine and now fuelled by a sample of Zorg's Zenith. The rocket stood ready on the makeshift launchpad. The air whispered with nervous excitement, anticipation thick as the bog mist clinging to their boots.
As Aoife, her fingers trembling slightly, flicked the ignition switch, the miniature Spudnik coughed and sputtered. A collective gasp rippled through the crew, followed by a tense silence. Then, with a shudder and a roar that echoed across the bog, the mini-rocket lurched upwards.
It wasn't graceful. It wasn't elegant. But it flew. Spurred by Zorg's Zenith, a blue vapour trail left behind like a celestial scarf, the miniature Spudnik sputtered its way towards the heavens. Finny whooped, Sheebie punched the air, and even Leaky cracked a broad grin.
The crew, their voices hoarse from cheers and panicked shouts of encouragement, watched as their mini-Spudnik reached its apogee, a speck of defiance against the vast canvas of the sky. Then, with a gentle wobble, it began its descent, the blue vapour trailing longer, stretching like a tether back to the bog.

As the mini-Spudnik settled back onto the earth with a soft thud, a wave of elation washed over them. Zorg, his face crinkled in a satisfied smile, accepted their exuberant congratulations with a nonchalant shrug. "Told you it was the right spud in the right barrel," he rumbled, his voice as earthy as the bog itself.

The test was a resounding success. Zorg's Zenith, a potent brew of potato magic and moonshine mystique, had proven its worth. Spudnik, the recently grounded dream, now had wings, fuelled by celestial elixir and the unwavering spirit of Ballymuckmore.

Walking back towards the village, bathed in the golden light of dawn, the crew discussed the logistics of producing enough Zenith to power their full-sized Spudnik. It was a daunting task, one that would require late nights, desperate measures, and possibly a few more whispered deals with the leprechauns. But the fear that had threatened to extinguish their dreams was replaced by a fierce determination, a shared belief that even the most improbable dreams could take flight from the bog.

Ballymuckmore, ever the village of surprises, had swapped its floral camouflage for a cloak of moonshine magic. The Bonanza, painted with children's dreams and now inspired by legend, stood poised on the launchpad, its rusty skin vibrating with the promise of interstellar travel. The laughter of the villagers, no longer masking their anxieties, mingled with the clink of tools, the cackle of metal being welded and the low murmur of Zorg's instructions.

Spudnik was no longer just a potato-powered dream; it was a vessel of hope, a testament to the unyielding spirit of a village on the edge of the bog. And with Zorg's Zenith whispering its celestial promises, Ballymuckmore was ready to reach for the stars, propelled by lunacy, laughter, and a legendary drop of moonshine magic.

Leaky's Luminous Mind

Leaky O'Sullivan wasn't your average Ballymuckmore boy. While his peers chased sheep and dreamed of bountiful potato harvests, Leaky's gaze was perpetually fixed on the intricate dance of raindrops on windowpanes, the mesmerising swirl of smoke rising from the hearth, and the curious way sunlight painted patterns on the worn floorboards. His world was a kaleidoscope of questions, each one a seed yearning to be planted in the fertile soil of his curiosity.
Unlike the boisterous laughter of Finny and the quiet wisdom of Sheebie, Leaky's world was filled with whispered theories and makeshift experiments. He'd spend hours dissecting wildflowers, their delicate petals revealing intricate structures unseen by the naked eye. He'd build contraptions from sticks and stones, powered by the wind and his boundless imagination, each one a testament to his yearning to understand the hidden workings of the world.
The villagers, bless their hearts, didn't quite understand. "Why waste your time on such foolishness, Leaky?" they'd say, shaking their heads. "There's no fortune to be found in daydreams and tinkering."
But Leaky wasn't interested in fortune. He craved knowledge, a deeper understanding of the forces that shaped the world around him. The rolling hills of Ballymuckmore might have been his home, but his mind yearned to explore the unseen, the microscopic wonders hidden within the everyday.
His sanctuary was the dusty attic, a treasure trove of forgotten curiosities – a chipped telescope, a tarnished compass, a stack of leather-bound books with faded ink whispering tales of faraway lands and forgotten discoveries. He devoured them,

each page igniting a new spark in his mind, a new question to ponder.

One starlit night, as he lay sprawled on the attic floor, a book on the wonders of electricity fell open, revealing a diagram of a simple battery. Leaky stared, mesmerised. The idea that everyday objects could hold such hidden power, that metal and acid could spark a flame, captivated him. He had to see it for himself.

The next morning, his pockets overflowing with scavenged materials – copper wire, potatoes, rusty nails – Leaky set to work. He followed the diagram, his brow furrowed in concentration, his tongue sticking out in determination. Finally, with a trembling hand, he connected the last wire. A spark, a flicker, and then… a dim light glowed from a scrap of metal, fuelled by the humble potato.

Tears welled up in Leaky's eyes, not of sadness, but of awe and overwhelming joy. This wasn't just a flickering light; it was a testament to the power of curiosity, a tangible proof that even the most fantastical ideas could be brought to life.

From that day on, Leaky's reputation as the village oddball was solidified. His pockets were perpetually filled with wires and gears, his hands stained with the grime of experimentation. But beneath the eccentricities, a brilliant mind bloomed, quickened by an insatiable thirst for knowledge.

He knew his path wouldn't be easy. Ballymuckmore, with its traditions and expectations, might not always understand his pursuits. But as he stood in the attic, the faint glow of his potato-powered light illuminating his face, he felt a newfound resolve. The world was a vast and wondrous place, and Leaky, the boy with a head full of questions and a heart full of curiosity, wouldn't let anyone dim his luminous mind. He was ready to embark on his own journey of discovery, one experiment, one invention, one spark of understanding at a time.

His introduction to the ancient art of making potcheen came as a bit of a surprise.

Leaky didn't mean to get kidnapped. One minute he was tinkering with his latest contraption - a potato-powered telegraph (don't ask, it was a work in progress) - the next, a rough hand clamped over his mouth and a gruff voice whispered, "Quiet, lad. You're coming with us."

Disoriented, hooded and slightly terrified, Leaky found himself bundled into a cart, bumping along a muddy path under the cloak of night. His captors remained eerily silent. His mind raced with fantastical possibilities – smugglers, leprechauns, perhaps even the mythical Banshee herself.

The familiar stench of peat smoke and overflowing ashtrays hit Leaky like a rogue wave as he stumbled into the dimly lit back room and was lowered onto a chair. He blinked as the hood, an old potato sack, was removed from his head and his eyes adjusted to the warm glow of a dimly lit room.

"Leaky O'Sullivan, boy genius," boomed a gravelly voice. "We've heard of your thirst for knowledge, your knack for tinkering."

Leaky, his heart pounding. "Wh-what do you want? Anyway, it wasn't me, it was one of the big lads and he ran away"

"We need new blood, lad," the voice chuckled.

Leaky swallowed hard. Vampires.

His captures removed their cloaks.

He could hear the chatter of voices in another room, muffled through the heavy door. The occasional sound of glasses clinking. He was in the Pub with No Name.

"My name is Seamus O'Flaherty"

"I know, you drink with me Da"

"We are the 'Brotherhood of the Bog', keepers of the ancient craft." Seamus continued, "As I said, we need new blood and what we want, what we need, is you"
Leaky swallowed hard again.
Seamus explained their predicament: the Brotherhood, once a thriving group of potcheen makers, had dwindled. Their knowledge, passed down through generations, was in danger of being lost. They needed someone young, sharp, and most importantly, someone with a thirst for knowledge like Leaky. Leaky's initial shock gave way to a mix of fear and...interest. potcheen, the illicit moonshine whispered about in hushed tones, the very symbol of Ballymuckmore's rebellious spirit. Could they be serious? Were they offering him...an apprenticeship?
"What do you expect of me?" he asked cautiously.
The man gestured towards the bubbling copper contraption in the corner. "Learn. Observe. Master the art of crafting the finest potcheen this side of the Shannon. Become one of us."
"Will you join us?" he said, extending a hand.
Leaky hesitated, then grasped the hand and stepped into a world of forbidden knowledge, shrouded in secrecy and maintained by the potent spirit of rebellion. His kidnapping, although unwanted, had become an unexpected gateway to a world he never dared dream of entering. And as the men of the Brotherhood unveiled the secrets of their craft, Leaky knew his life would never be the same. The boy with an insatiable thirst for knowledge was about to embark on a journey that would redefine him, blurring the lines between science, tradition, and the illicit allure of the forbidden.

Of Kings and Legends

The morning mist lay thick on the ground as Leaky trudged across the dew-kissed fields, the worn leather satchel containing Zorg's Zenith still blueprints slung across his shoulder. His destination: Cormac O'Neill's forge, a few villages over and shrouded in its own legend of fiery tempers and impeccable craftsmanship.

Leaky, never one for unnecessary dramatics, had hoped for a quick exchange: designs presented, parts forged, a muttered thank you, and a brisk return to his shed. But as he entered the forge, the rhythmic clang of hammer on metal and the scent of burning coal instantly dispelled any notions of a swift transaction.

Cormac O'Neill, a burly man with arms like tree trunks and a beard that could rival Santa's, looked up from his work, his bushy eyebrows rising in surprise. "Leaky O'Sullivan, as I live and breathe," he rumbled, his voice deep as the forge itself. "What brings you to my humble establishment?"

"I have need of some specialist parts that are beyond my skills at tinkering"

"Is this another of your 'experiments' in liquid refinement?" Cormac smiled.

"Oh, this on another level altogether." Leaky laid the detailed sketches on the workbench.

Cormac squinted at the designs, his coke smeared face creased in concentration. A silence stretched between them, thick with the anticipation of the blacksmith's verdict.

"Would this be official Brotherhood of the Bog work ?"

"Er, no, but how do you know about the Brotherhood, it's supposed to be a secret society? " Leaky was surprised.

"Who do you think has been building their contraptions all these years, Leprechauns ?"

Cormac continue looking over the plans. Finally, he chuckled, a sound like rocks tumbling down a mountainside. "Building a still with Zorg, are you? I'd recognise that tinker and his contraptions anywhere..." He shook his head, a hint of a smile playing on his lips. "But I can't say I'm surprised. You O'Sullivans always had a penchant for the unorthodox."

Leaky squinted at the burly blacksmith as he peered over his shoulder, the blacksmith's calloused finger tracing the intricate design of the condenser coil.

"This here," Cormac rumbled, his voice low like the roar of the furnace behind him, "it's clever, young O'Sullivan, but not very efficient. Let me show you a little trick I learned from a traveling tinkerer myself, years ago..."

Intrigue sparked in Leaky's eyes. He'd come expecting a gruff exchange, not a masterclass in metalworking. He shifted his satchel, the worn leather straps biting into his shoulder, but his attention was fully captured.

Cormac chuckled, a sound like rocks tumbling down a mountainside. "This Zorg of yours, he has grand ideas, that much is true. But sometimes, simpler is better. See this coil here? All these fancy twists and turns, they just slow down the vapour flow. We want it smooth, like water over a riverbed."

Cormac reached for a length of stainless steel, its surface dull with a coat of dust. He tossed it into the furnace, the orange glow instantly igniting its edges. As the metal heated, its colour shifted, morphing from dull red to vibrant orange.

"Now, watch closely," Cormac said, his voice gaining a quiet intensity. He pulled the glowing steel from the furnace with tongs, sparks showering the floor. With practiced ease, he hammered the metal on the anvil, shaping it with precise blows. The clangs resonated through the forge, each one accompanied by a hiss as he plunged the metal into a bucket of water.

Slowly, a new shape emerged – a simpler coil, with fewer twists and turns but a wider diameter. "See, lad," Cormac explained, wiping sweat from his brow, "less clutter, more flow. This'll cool the vapour quicker, give you a smoother, cleaner spirit."

Leaky ran his fingers over the still-warm metal, impressed by its simple elegance. "But this won't fit the existing design," he said, worry creeping into his voice.

Cormac winked, a mischievous glint in his eye. "Ah, now that's where the fun part comes in. We improvise, lad. We adapt. Zorg might have the fancy ideas, but a good smith knows how to make them work in the real world."

He spent the next hour guiding Leaky, sharing his knowledge of metal properties, heat treatment, and the subtle art of bending metal to one's will. Leaky, a quick learner, grasped the concepts with enthusiasm, his initial apprehension transforming into a newfound respect for the blacksmith's craft.

As the sun dipped below the horizon, casting long shadows through the forge, the missing parts were complete. They weren't just functional; they were works of art, their simple lines imbued with the quiet magic of the forge and the shared knowledge of two unlikely collaborators.

"There you go, lad," Cormac said, handing Leaky the carefully crafted pieces. "Now go finish your contraption, and remember, sometimes the best inventions are the ones that don't overthink things."

Leaky nodded, his heart warmed by the unexpected camaraderie. He left the forge not just with improved parts, but with a newfound appreciation for the wisdom hidden within the

clanging rhythm of the hammer and the fiery heart of the blacksmith. As he walked into the cool evening air, he knew the Zenith still wouldn't just be a testament to Zorg's vision, but to the unexpected collaboration that had brought it to life, forever etched in the simple elegance of the blacksmith's touch.
Leaky's shed, usually a haven of whirring gears and half-finished contraptions, was transformed into a makeshift alchemical laboratory. The pungent aroma of Zorg's Zenith hung thick in the air, mingling with the earthy scent of peat and the metallic tang of welding torches.
Leaky handed the satchel containing the new parts to Zorg. He carefully lifted each piece out and inspected it closely before placing it purposefully on the table.
"These are good. Better than I designed" Zorg paused. "I see Cormac O'Neill's handiwork here" He turned the part in his hand slowly, examining every angle. "Yes, definitely Cormac's work"
"I told you I was going to see Cormac when I left this morning"
"Oh, did you? Ah, yes you did. " Zorg put the piece on the table and turned back to construction site.
Leaky, worked tirelessly alongside Zorg to expand the humble still into a production line worthy of Spudnik's ambitions, although he did wonder how many pinches of salt he should take with what Zorg was telling him.
As they toiled, the fire in the still crackled and whispered, and Zorg, warmed by both peat fire and potato punch, regaled Leaky with tales of his past. He spoke of moonlit nights spent brewing in hollowed-out fairy rings, of leprechauns dancing jigs atop barrels of bubbling mash, and of mischievous banshees who, with a single giggle, could turn a perfectly clear potcheen into a frothing, purple brew with the kick of a banshee's wail.

Leaky listened with rapt attention. He always did love a story well told.

He had always suspected a connection between Ireland, his beloved potcheen, and the little folk who flitted through the legends and fireside whispers of his childhood. Now, with Zorg's tales weaving a tapestry of magic and moonshine, the veil between myth and reality seemed to shimmer and thin. Zorg, his face etched with wrinkles like a road map to forgotten moonshine trails, chuckled at Leaky's apparent wide-eyed wonder.

"Aye," he rumbled, taking a swig from a battered flask that seemed to magically refill itself, "the wee folk have a taste for the good stuff. And they've got secrets, lad, secrets about the land, the skies, and the very fabric of the universe, all locked away in their wee jars of moonbeam and starlight."

He leaned in, his voice dropping to a conspiratorial whisper. "Once upon a time, I almost married the leprechaun king's daughter. A fiery one she was, with eyes the colour of emeralds and a laugh that could set potatoes dancing. We were courting, see, stealing kisses under the moon and sharing stories by the firelight. But the king, a cantankerous old soul with a beard like a tangled brier patch, wasn't too keen on his daughter marrying a simple potcheen-maker."

Leaky smiled. Zorg's tales were even taller than the very best he could conjure up. He played along, begging for more. Zorg, with a mischievous glint in his eye, stretched the story out like a piece of taffy, each pause punctuated by the gurgle of the still and the clink of Leaky's tools. He spoke of riddles exchanged in the twilight, of tests of strength and wit set by the leprechaun king, and of a final challenge that involved brewing the most potent, moon-touched potcheen the world had ever known.

In the end, Leaky learned, Zorg had won the daughter's hand, but the Leprechaun King, in a fit of stubborn pride, whisked her away to the Otherworld before the vows could be exchanged. Zorg, heartbroken but never defeated, poured his grief and longing into his potcheen, creating a brew that could make the stars dance and whisper secrets of the cosmos and swore to never supply the Leprechaun King with a single drop. And that, Leaky discovered, was the very brew that now bubbled in their new still, the fuel that would propel Spudnik towards the heavens, a testament to love, loss, and the magic that simmered beneath the surface of Ireland's green hills.

As the dawn broke, painting the sky with streaks of orange and gold, Leaky and Zorg stood back from their creation, a gleaming contraption that hummed with the promise of potato-powered flight. The tale of the leprechaun king's daughter, a wisp of smoke on the morning breeze, had woven itself into the very fabric of their endeavour. Spudnik was no longer just a rocket; it was a vessel carrying dreams, myths, and the undying spirit of a village filled with laughter, lunacy, and a drop of legendary, moon-touched potcheen.

The day stretched before them, filled with the clatter of tools, the gurgle of the still, and the whispered promises of the stars. Leaky, his eyes shining with the light of a thousand moonshine-fuelled tales, knew that their journey wasn't just about reaching space; it was about embracing the magic that coursed through their land, their hearts, and their very potcheen. Spudnik, a potato-powered dream born in a smoking shed and propelled by a leprechaun king's heartbreak, was poised to take flight, carrying with it the laughter, the lore, and the boundless spirit of Ballymuckmore. And as the first rays of the sun kissed the bog, Leaky and Zorg, two unlikely partners in lunacy and moonshine, raised a toast.

"To the impossible dream, Leaky!" Zorg boomed, his weathered face crinkled in a smile. The flask in his hand, chipped and scarred like an old warrior, clinked merrily against Leaky's old tin cup, the metallic chime echoing through the shed.

The still, now a monstrous contraption of pipes and bubbling tanks, hissed and gurgled like a contented dragon, belching out plumes of purple-tinged steam that danced amongst the rafters. It was a far cry from Leaky's humble contraption, but under Zorg's tutelage and an endless supply of potatoes, it churned out Zenith with the efficiency of a leprechaun gold mine.

Love Blossoms in the Spud Fields

Aoife perched on a rickety stool in Finny's cluttered workshop, the scent of sawdust and engine grease clinging to the air like a familiar blanket. Sunlight streamed through the grime-coated window, illuminating a constellation of odd sized tools and half-finished contraptions. In the centre, sprawled across the workbench, lay the blueprints for Spudnik, an intricate network of lines and calculations dancing across faded parchment.
Finny, his brow furrowed in concentration, traced a trajectory with a calloused finger. "See here, Aoife," he said, his voice animated. "If we adjust the fuel intake by five percent, we can squeeze out an extra mile or two. Every wee bit counts, you know."
Aoife nodded, her heart doing its own peculiar orbit within her chest. She wanted to laugh at his earnest dedication, to tell him that a potato-fuelled rocket wouldn't be so concerned with fuel efficiency, but the words caught in her throat like butterflies tangled in a spiderweb.
"Finny," she began, her voice barely above a whisper. His head snapped up, his eyes, the colour of a summer sky, meeting hers. For a moment, the workshop vanished, replaced by a swirling kaleidoscope of green and blue. Then, he grinned, a familiar, sun-warmed grin that made Aoife's stomach flip like a spud in a hot pan.
"What is it, Aoife? Did you crack the trajectory code?"
Disappointment pricked at her. Of course, all he saw was her as his little sister, the brainy one who could whip up equations on a whim. But before she could retreat, her own words surprised her.
"No," she blurted out, her voice surprisingly firm. "I just… I wanted to say…"

She faltered, her cheeks burning the same shade as the sunset sky outside. The butterflies in her stomach had taken flight, fluttering erratically against the bars of her throat. Finny's brow furrowed, a crease forming between his eyes.

"Say what?" he prompted, his voice gentle, concern replacing the earlier spark of excitement.

Aoife took a deep breath, the workshop spinning around her. "I wanted to say... that I really admire you, Finny."

The words felt heavy, inadequate, like pebbles thrown at a mountain. But as she spoke them, a tiny seed of hope blossomed in her chest. Maybe, just maybe, they were enough.

Finny's smile faltered, replaced by a look of dawning comprehension. His cheeks, usually the colour of tanned leather, flushed a deeper shade. He looked at her, really looked at her, for the first time not as his little sister, but as a young woman, her eyes shimmering with unspoken emotions.

"Aoife," he began, his voice rough, hesitant, "I... I always thought of you as... well... as like my little sister."

Aoife's heart stuttered. Had she misread everything? Was this just a cruel cosmic joke and destined for failure?

But then, Finny's hand reached out, tentatively brushing a strand of hair from her eyes. His touch sent a jolt of electricity through her, a current more powerful than any Zenith fuel.

"But," he continued, his voice barely above a whisper, "maybe... maybe it's time I started thinking of you differently."

Aoife's breath hitched. Was this really happening? Was Finny actually seeing her, the real her, not just the equations and calculations that danced in her head?

A slow smile bloomed on her face, as radiant as a potato flower bathed in moonlight. The butterflies in her stomach settled, finally finding a home in the warmth of his gaze.

"Maybe," she echoed, her voice soft but brimming with newfound confidence.

The workshop, once a cluttered haven for improbable dreams, transformed into a universe of possibilities. The blueprints on the workbench faded, replaced by a blueprint for a future they could build together, fuelled not by potatoes and moonshine, but by something far more potent: the spark of a shared dream, the whispered promise of something more.

As the sun started its exit below the horizon, painting the sky in hues of orange and gold, Finny and Aoife sat shoulder to shoulder, their hands brushing under the workbench. They didn't need to speak; the unspoken words hung in the air, thick and sweet like the scent of bog berries after a summer rain. Spudnik, once just a potato-powered moonshot, became a symbol of something more. It was a testament to the impossible dream, to the laughter and lunacy that dared to reach for the stars. But most of all, it was a promise, a whispered secret shared between a girl who dared to dream and a boy who finally saw her, not just as his little sister, but as the girl who made his own heart do a celestial jig. The setting sun cast long shadows across the workshop, but its waning light did nothing to dim the glow in Aoife's eyes.

A laugh, light and airy like wind chimes on a summer breeze, escaped her lips. "And maybe," she said, her fingers intertwining with his under the workbench, "I'm the one who needs more than a big brother sometimes."

The air crackled with unspoken confessions, a delicious tension that mirrored the spark between the electrodes of their unfinished rocket. For a moment, they simply sat in the silence, the warmth of their hands chasing away the chill of the approaching night. The blueprints on the workbench, once a

road map to the stars, seemed to recede, replaced by a constellation of unspoken promises etched in the sky above.
"So," Finny broke the silence, his voice a low rumble, "where does this leave us, spud-scientist?"
Aoife's heart skipped a beat. "Well," she countered, her smile mischievous, "I suppose it depends. Are you still willing to let me be your co-pilot on this crazy journey, even if I come with extra baggage?"
Finny, a grin mirroring hers, pulled her closer. "Always," he whispered, his breath warm against her ear. "As long as you promise to share the steering wheel, and maybe, just maybe, teach me a thing or two about celestial jigs."
A playful smirk danced on Sheebie's lips as she surveyed the scene from the doorway. "Well, look at yer," she drawled, her voice laden with good-natured amusement. "The spud-whiz finally confessed her undying passion to the spud-king!"
Aoife, cheeks tinged with a blushing pink, spluttered a denial. "Undying passion? I just… told him I admired him!"
Sheebie chuckled, a low rumble that echoed the gentle tremor in Aoife's heart. "Oh, come on, Aoife," she teased. "We haven't all gone blind. The way you two mooned at each other over calculations it's a wonder Father Dougal hasn't had you in for his 'talk'"
Aoife sighed, a mixture of relief and embarrassment washing over her. "So you knew?"
Sheebie's smirk softened. "We all did, love," she admitted, her voice now as gentle as the breeze rustling through the bog-berry bushes. "Except maybe yourselves, you pair of oblivious boggers. But we figured you'd work it out in your own good time, spud by spud."
A wave of warmth washed over Aoife. It was somehow comforting to know her fumbling attempts at love hadn't gone

completely unnoticed. "Thanks, Sheebie," she mumbled, reaching for her friend's hand.

Sheebie squeezed her hand gently. "Well, fear not, love struck spud-scientist," she said with a wink. "The skies might be full of celestial wonders, but there's also a pretty spectacular fireworks display happening right here on Earth, courtesy of Finny and you. Don't let the blueprints block your view."

Aoife's heart soared. Sheebie's words were a gentle nudge, a reminder that while Spudnik was indeed an incredible dream, the love blossoming between her and Finny was a whole other universe waiting to be explored.

With a grateful smile, Aoife turned back to Finny, the blueprints on the workbench suddenly seeming far less important. The stars could wait; right now, she had a constellation of feelings dancing in her eyes, and a potato-powered love story waiting to be written.

As Finny's gaze met hers, the workshop dissolved, replaced by a universe lit not by moonshine or potato flames, but by the warm glow of shared dreams and whispered promises. In that moment, Aoife knew, Spudnik might have been the vessel taking them to the stars, but it was love, their own clumsy, Ballymuckmore style of love, that would truly fuel their journey, lighting the way through the vast and wondrous expanse of their future together.

The village of Ballymuckmore, forever imprinted with the echoes of lunacy, could have never imagined the celestial love story blossoming within its heart. But as the stars winked their approval from above, Spudnik became more than just a rocket; it became a symbol of courage, of dreaming big, and of love taking flight, defying gravity and reaching for the impossible, one small step at a time.

Skeptic Tanks

Ah, Wednesday, the thrilling midpoint of the week, or as Laoise at the Post Office called it, "Just another day in the slow lane." But let's be honest, every day was a tranquil oasis in the world of postage

It had been a while since Laoise had settled onto her trusty stool behind the counter, meticulously filling out yet another bureaucratic form, making sure every "T" was crossed and every "I" dotted. As for that particular form, well, she hadn't really given it a second thought. After all, paperwork was about as thrilling as watching paint dry on a wet Monday in Ballymuckmore.

The rhythmic chug of a diesel engine and the repetitive beep from a lorry reversing brought the memories flooding back.

The note pinned to the door cheerfully announced Laoise's temporary absence, promising her return "in a bit." How long a "bit" was, however, remained as mysterious as the ingredients in Leaky's moonshine. With a nonchalant click, she locked up shop and sauntered off down the cobbled street, her destination set for Bonanza

A burly lorry driver, clipboard in hand, swaggered through the large side doors into Bonanza, his eyes scanning the room amazed at the amount of junk there was lying around.

"Delivery for BSP, where do you want these putting?" he announced, his voice booming.

The Spudnik crew glanced up from their task of sorting through rocket components, exchanging bewildered glances at the unexpected arrival. "BSP?" echoed Finny, scratching his head in confusion. "I don't recall ordering anything. Did any of you?" he queried, turning to the others for confirmation, their faces reflecting the same puzzlement.

The crew's bewilderment deepened. Septic tanks? In Bonanza? It made no sense. Yet, there they stood, two imposing plastic giants demanding an explanation.
Just then, Laoise strolled in, wiping her hands on her apron. "Delivery for me, is it?" she inquired, her eyes widening at the sight of the two hulking tanks on the flatbed. The driver, surprised, checked his clipboard again. "Aye, that's right, ma'am. Two septic tanks for BSP."
"Just drop them over there, "she pointed to a clear spot near to the large open doors, "That'll be fine".
The Spudnik crew's confusion deepened. "Septic tanks?" Sheebie whispered, eyes wide. "But why...? Why here ....?"
Aoife, was being her usual quiet and observant self, stood frozen, her gaze fixed on the tanks. A slow realisation dawned on her face, a smile spreading into a mischievous grin. She nudged Finny, her voice barely a whisper, "You know what these are, don't you?"
"A bog in the bog?" Finny, still clueless.
"Fuel tanks, Finny. They're Fuel tanks!"
It wasn't too long before Leaky and Sheebie saw the potential being deposited on the ground outside of Bonanza.
As the lorry pulled away, the crew stood staring at the new additions to Spudnik's parts list.
"Laoise," Finny stammered, his voice barely a whisper, "are you telling me..."
Laoise winked, chuckling at the absurdity of the situation. "Well, you see," she began, her voice warm and conspiratorial, "Constable O'Toole mentioned your project and that you were in a bit of pickle with regards to sourcing large tanks. So, I thought, maybe, one tank is as good as another. Now, I may not be an expert in rocket science, but I do know a thing or two about forms and grants, and let me tell you, a septic tank grant

can be surprisingly, er, versatile, if you know how to bend the rules a little."

A mischievous glint twinkled in her eyes. "So, I thought, 'Why not use my skills to help you crazy Spudnik dreamers out?' Besides," she added with a wink, "a little harmless bureaucratic bending never hurt anyone, right?"

The crew, still buzzing from the revelation and relief, erupted in cheers and laughter.

Finny, ever the jokester, bowed dramatically. "Lady Laoise, you are a saint! A bureaucratic ninja, a paperwork sorceress! We are eternally in your debt!" he proclaimed with a flourish, his words met with enthusiastic nods and applause from his fellow Spudnik comrades.

Sheebie, more reserved but equally grateful, offered a small smile and a heartfelt, "Thank you, Laoise. This is a huge help."

Leaky, his eyes shining with newfound determination, adjusted his goggles. "This changes everything! Now we can truly focus on getting Spudnik built."

Aoife, her smile mirroring Leaky's, added, "And who knows, maybe this is just the first of many... 'misunderstandings' that work in our favour."

Laoise raised an eyebrow, a playful smile playing on her lips. "Don't tempt fate, dear Aoife. But let's just say, I'm always happy to help a worthy cause, even if it means stretching the truth a tad."

" BSP " Sheebie puzzled, "I've never heard of a company called BSP"

"Are you sure you haven't dear Sheebie. BSP..." Laoise winked, "or, the Ballymuckmore Space Program " she said as she turned to stroll back to her Post Office.

By the time the laughter had subsided, Laoise was once again ensconced behind her counter in the Post office.

The crew, buzzing with the unexpected fuel-tank windfall, turned their attention to the behemoths now dominating Bonanza. Two dark green plastic septic tanks might not have been their first choice for rocket fuel storage, but they were here, and ingenuity was Ballymuckmore's middle name.

Finny, ever the optimist, thumped one of the tanks with a fist. "Alright, lads and lass! Let's turn these septic stinkers into space-worthy fuel pods!"

Aoife, the newly appointed rocket engineer, took charge. "First things first, we need to seal those existing openings. Duct tape and wishful thinking will not get us off the bog."

Sheebie, the quiet observer, piped up, "And we can mount them vertically inside Spudnik. Valves at the top for filling and the bottom to feed the engine... hmm, that might actually work."

Leaky, his brow furrowed in thought, added, "But these tanks are designed for liquids, not pressurised fuel. We'll need to reinforce them somehow." He paused, staring at the tanks. "hmm, I think you're right, it might actually work."

Finny clattered about in a pile of what some people would call junk, but the spudnik crew call unsorted components, and pulled out a bunch of hydraulic hoses.

Aoife's eyebrows shot up, a playful smirk dancing on her lips. "Hot? Or just... ridiculously resourceful?" she flirted, eyeing Finny with a mixture of amusement and admiration.

Finny, oblivious to the double entendre, grinned and held up a hose triumphantly. "These bad boys are built to handle the pressure of a farm tractor lifting its own weight in spuds, Spudnik's fuel will be a doddle!" He shook the hoses dramatically, sending a spray of dust into the air. "And somewhere in that pile, " pointing to the mountain for scavenged farm parts, "are what these connect to"

Sheebie, who had been quietly sketching potential designs, spoke up. "If we use these hoses, they might require additional supports and pressure regulators to function optimally."

Finny grinned, his confidence restored. "See? Ballymuckmore magic! We turn septic tanks into fuel pods and farmyard scraps into rocket parts! Spudnik's gonna take flight, one ingenious idea at a time!"

The septic tanks, once the punchline for hilarious misunderstanding, were now being transformed into a springboard for their collective ingenuity. The task was daunting, the unknowns aplenty, but the spirit of Ballymuckmore crackled in the air. They had a fuel solution, they had each other, and they had the unwavering belief that even the most absurd beginnings could lead to the most extraordinary journeys. With laughter, determination, and a healthy dose of duct tape, they would be ready to fill those septic tanks with the fuel that would propel their dreams towards the stars.

Sabotage

Ballymuckmore buzzed like a beehive disturbed by a rogue spud. The Beautiful Ireland competition, once a distant rumble, had exploded into a full-blown phenomenon, the village transformed into a whimsical stage for tourists and curious onlookers. Busloads of wide-eyed city folk poured in, cameras clutched like talismans, their eyes wide with the promise of quaint charm and rustic beauty.
Agnes McSweeney, proprietor of the Pub with No Name, couldn't wipe the smile off her face. Her normally sleepy establishment throbbed with the chatter of visitors, the air thick with the aroma of bacon and sausage, the clinking of mugs filled with all manner of Agnes's legendary brews. The full Irish breakfast, once a local delicacy, had become a must-have for tourists, each bite a testament to the village's hidden culinary treasures.
But the tourists weren't the only unusual arrivals. Whispers of a blue vapour trail over the bog had drifted through the ether, attracting a new breed of visitors: the tin-foil hat brigade. Men with eyes like the saucers they hoped to uncover and muttered pronouncements about extraterrestrial spuds stalked the bog, their antennae twitching for the slightest hint of the mythical Spudnik.
Finny, usually nonchalant, was on high alert. He and Aoife, their heads still spinning from their inevitable confession, knew they had to keep Spudnik a secret, at least until the competition. The last thing they needed was a bunch of conspiracy theorists poking around their potato-fuelled rocket. Leaky, however, was tickled pink by the attention. He regaled the tin-foil brigade with embellished tales of Zorg's Zenith, weaving fantastical yarns of potato-powered moon cows and

leprechaun-built moon rovers. The tourists, half-believing, half-amused, ate it up, adding fuel to the fire of Ballymuckmore's lunacy.

Sheebie, saw a silver lining in the chaos. With the village on the map, she envisioned a future filled with tourists, sheep-themed merchandise, and maybe even a woolly theme park. Aoife worried about the ethics of exploiting their lunacy for profit, but even she couldn't deny the potential to bring Ballymuckmore out of its boggy slumber.

As the days flew by, the competition heated up. The other villages, initially amused by Ballymuckmore's potato-powered antics, grew nervous as their carefully crafted displays of floral arches and twee cottages paled in comparison to the village's chaotic charm. The tourists, tired of predictable perfection, flocked to Ballymuckmore, drawn by the promise of laughter, moonshine, and the possibility of having an extra-terrestrial encounter.

Agnes's pub, the official HQ of the competition, was also a melting pot of tourists, villagers, and conspiracy theorists, all united by their shared love of Guinness, potatoes, lunacy, and the unknown. The air crackled with anticipation, a delicious blend of nervous energy and excitement.

Although the friendly competition has stirred ancient rivalries that needed to be redressed.

In the hushed predawn hours, while Ballymuckmore slept beneath a starry veil, shadows crept down the boggy lane from the neighbouring village of Kilmuckety. Armed with pliers, mischievous grins, and an unhealthy dose of competitive spirit, a trio of Kilmuckety lads had come to "adjust" the Bonanza, ensuring their own village's victory in the Beautiful Ireland competition.

Little did they know, however, that Ballymuckmore had their own, furry, four-legged security system. Seamus, the resident sheepdog, his nose twitching with canine intuition, caught the scent of foreign intruders on the breeze. With a startled bark, he woke his trusty companion, Seamus the donkey, whose ears perked up like potato sprouts in a downpour.

The livestock, sensing Seamus's unease, stirred in their pens. Sheep, normally docile as clouds, baaed with suspicion. Chickens, usually content to peck and squawk, clucked an insistent alarm. Ballymuckmore was about to become a barnyard symphony of discontent.

The Kilmuckety boys, oblivious to the impending furry hurricane, reached the Bonanza. One burly lad, Micko, began fiddling with the support lines, his accomplice, Seamus (no relation to the sheepdog, or the donkey), held the flashlight, and third, Kevin, kept lookout, shivering despite the muggy air. Suddenly, a flurry of movement caught Kevin's eye. Through the dim moonlight, he saw a herd of fluffy white shapes bearing down on them, eyes glinting like marbles in the night. "Sheep!" he shrieked, his voice a comical falsetto.

Panic seized the trio. Micko dropped his pliers, sending them clattering against the metal hull. Seamus (flashlight) tripped over Kevin, sending the beam dancing wildly across the bog. And amongst the chaos, Seamus the sheepdog, his tail wagging with canine glee, led the charge, his flock trailing behind like a woolly tidal wave.

The bog, normally quiet and serene, erupted in a cacophony of bleats, barks, and the thunderous hooves of a galloping donkey. The sheep, normally content to graze, head-butted the intruders' legs with surprising force. Seamus (sheepdog), nipped at their ankles, his playful barks morphing into growls. And Seamus (donkey), usually stoic, brayed a triumphant call that echoed across the moonlit bog.

The Kilmuckety lads, overwhelmed by the furry onslaught, stumbled and bumbled, their sabotage plans dissolving into slapstick comedy.

Micko fell, face first, into a puddle of questionable origin, Seamus (flashlight) tripped over a bale of hay, and Kevin found himself singled out by a particularly determined sheep named Agnes. Agnes, a veteran of countless turf wars with Kilmuckety sheep, saw Kevin as a trespasser in need of a good fleecing. She charged, head lowered, horns glinting under the moon, her woolly bulk propelled by a grudge thicker than bog mud.

Seamus (flashlight), tangled in a hay bale, flailed wildly, the beam of light painting the night sky with squiggly constellations. His panicked shouts bounced off the silent Bonanza, sounding like a banshee with laryngitis.

Kevin, legs pumping like pistons, weaved through the sheep stampede, nimble as a ferret dodging the hay bales. He ducked under Seamus (donkey) causing a startled bray, narrowly avoiding an encounter with its hooves.

Seamus (flashlight) freed himself from the hay bale and saw his opportunity to make a run for it. He headed straight for the gate, neatly side stepping Agnes, who was still pursuing Kevin. There, in his way stood the defiant Seamus (donkey). Their eyes met. Was that grin on Seamus (donkey)'s face? Do donkeys grin ? The cries Seamus (flashlight) emitted as he flew through the air were blood curdling.

Agnes, triggered by years of pent up Kilmuckety rivalry, was relentless. She rammed a hay bale into Kevin's path, sending him sprawling into a mud puddle, well, it looked like mud, but how the sheep turned away in horror, suggested otherwise.

Micko, who'd finally extricated himself from the bog mire, saw Kevin's predicament and let out a defiant bellow.
"Kilmuckety'!" he hollered, his cry echoing across the bog.
But Micko hadn't reckoned on Seamus (sheepdog). Seized by a sense of chivalry to uphold the honour of Ballymuckmore, Seamus launched himself at Micko, a furry missile guided by righteous indignation. He tackled Micko to the ground, a tangle of paws and teeth and bewildered yelps.
Kevin, seizing the opportunity while Agnes was distracted by Micko's outburst, scrambled to his feet, mud, at least it looked like mud, dripping from his ears and a sheepish look plastered on his face.
And then, the pièce de résistance. Seamus (sheepdog), having led the charge with the gusto of a four legged Viking warrior, reached the hapless trio. He stood before them, tail wagging furiously, a triumphant glint in his eyes. He barked once, a sharp, commanding bark that echoed across the field, silencing the cacophony. The sheep, emboldened by their leader's display, stopped their assault, forming a woolly circle around the intruders like a fluffy stockade.
Sheebie, who had been alerted by the commotion and armed with a broom and a fierce glare, apprehended the culprits with the ease, thanks to the work of Seamus (sheepdog). The lads, defeated and slightly bewildered and emitting an extremely unpalatable aroma, were handed over to Constable O'Toole, still in his pyjamas, who had also been woken by the commotion.
As the rising sun bathed the bog in a golden hue, Ballymuckmore emerged victorious, thanks to the valiant efforts of its livestock and Sheebie's quick thinking. The Kilmuckety lads, sporting bruises, mud-streaked clothes, and sheep-induced embarrassment, slinked away with their tails

between their legs and a flea in their ear, their dreams of conquest trampled by a flock of determined creatures.
The incident became another legend, a testament to the unexpected guardians of Ballymuckmore. Seamus the sheepdog, his tail held high, received a hero's welcome, complete with a couple of cold sausages and a belly rub from Agnes (Pub). Seamus the donkey, ever stoic, enjoyed a double portion of oats, his bray now a sound of victory rather than a call to arms.

Stargazing and Stardust Dreams

Aoife wasn't like the other children of Ballymuckmore. While they dreamt of prize sheep and bountiful potato harvests, her gaze was perpetually fixed on the vast expanse above. From the moment she could stand, her nights were spent sprawled on the soft grass, eyes wide with wonder as she devoured the tapestry of stars. The flickering flames of the hearth were replaced by the constellations, their ancient stories whispered on the wind.
Unlike Finny's infectious laughter and Sheebie's quiet wisdom, Aoife's world was filled with equations and nebulae, quasars and black holes. The dusty pages of her borrowed astronomy books held more allure than the latest gossip, and the rhythmic ticking of the grandfather clock was less captivating than the imagined ticking of a cosmic clock.
The villagers, bless their hearts, didn't quite understand. "Why waste your mind on stars, Aoife?" they'd say, shaking their heads. "There's no fortune to be made gazing at the sky."
But Aoife wasn't interested in fortune. She craved knowledge, understanding the universe's grand design, the invisible forces that held everything together. The rolling hills of Ballymuckmore might have been her home, but her spirit yearned for the infinite expanse beyond.
She spent her days devouring books, the library her sanctuary. The disapproving frowns from some villagers only fueled her determination. Every stolen glance at the sky, every whispered question about the cosmos, was a tiny rebellion against the expectations placed upon her.
One starlit night, as she lay beneath the shimmering Milky Way, a meteor streaked across the sky, leaving a trail of stardust in its wake. It was a sign, Aoife felt it in her bones.

This wasn't just a fleeting wish; it was a calling, a whisper urging her to chase her dreams, no matter how far they seemed. The next day, she approached Cormac O'Neill, the gruff blacksmith with a surprising twinkle in his eye. "Mr. O'Neill," she began, her voice trembling slightly, "I need your help building a telescope."

The blacksmith's eyes narrowed, skepticism battling with amusement as Aoife finished her passionate plea. "A telescope, you say? And what makes you think a simple village blacksmith like me can help you reach for the stars ?"

Aoife held his gaze, her chin jutting defiantly. "Because I've seen the way you work, Mr. O'Neill. You bend metal to your will, coaxing it into shapes that serve a purpose. Isn't that what a telescope does? Bends light to reveal what's hidden?"

A slow smile tugged at the blacksmith's lips. "Aye, there's some truth to that. But telescopes are delicate things, made by craftsmen in faraway lands with tools I've never seen."

"I know it won't be perfect," Aoife conceded, "but even a glimpse, Mr. O'Neill, just a glimpse of Jupiter's moons or Saturn's rings, would be enough to set my soul alight."

He studied her for a long moment, the firelight dancing in his eyes. "You have the fire in your belly, that much is clear. But fire alone won't build a telescope. You need knowledge, lass. Books, calculations, understanding how light behaves."

"I have the books," Aoife declared, patting her worn satchel. "And I'm a quick learner. I promise you, Mr. O'Neill, I'll study day and night. I'll work twice as hard as any apprentice you've ever had."

Cormac chuckled, the sound deep and rumbling. "Stubborn as a mule, that's what you are. But that might just be the kind of spirit needed to chase such lofty dreams."

He scratched his beard thoughtfully. "Alright, lass. I won't promise success, but I'll offer what I can. Tools, scraps of metal, and maybe a few pointers along the way. But remember, building this contraption will be as much about grit as it is about skill. Are you ready for blisters on your hands and grease under your fingernails?"

Aoife grinned, her eyes sparkling brighter than the stars above. "As ready as I'll ever be, Mr. O'Neill. Let's build a bridge to the stars, one hammer blow at a time."

And so, an unlikely partnership began. Aoife devoured the borrowed books, her mind swimming with diagrams and formulas. Cormac, gruff but patient, guided her through the practicalities, teaching her the properties of metal, the delicate touch needed to bend and shape without shattering. They scavenged for materials, transforming discarded lenses and rusty gears into the beginnings of their audacious dream.

The smithy, already a haven of clanging metal, now whispered calculations, and shared laughter. Aoife's initial frustration at setbacks only compounded her determination, while Cormac, witnessing her unwavering spirit, found himself drawn back to the forgotten dreams of his youth.

As the days turned into weeks, their creation slowly took shape. It wasn't the polished instrument Aoife had seen in her books, but it held a certain rustic charm, each seam and scratch a testament to their shared endeavour.

One crisp autumn night, with the finished telescope pointed towards the heavens, Aoife held her breath. As she peered through the neatly fashioned lens, slowly changing the focus until a gasp escaped her lips. Jupiter, with its swirling bands, hung suspended in the inky blackness, its moons like tiny pearls scattered around its celestial crown. Tears welled up in her eyes, not just from the cold night air, but from the overwhelming realisation of her dream, brought to life through sheer grit and determination. On that night, her world shifted on its axis.

Cormac, watching her silent awe, felt a warmth spread through his chest. He hadn't just helped build a telescope; he had ignited a passion, a spark that might one day illuminate the farthest reaches of the universe.

"See, lass?" he rumbled, a hint of pride in his voice. "Even a village blacksmith can help you touch the stars."

Aoife turned to him, her eyes shining with gratitude. "You did Mr O'Neill, you did"

"It wasn't just me lass, there's just as much of you in that telescope. See what a bit of determination and a load of elbow grease can achieve."

And as they stood side by side, blacksmith and dreamer, beneath the endless tapestry of the night sky, they knew this was just the beginning. The telescope, a testament to their unlikely partnership, was more than just a tool; it was a symbol of their shared journey, a reminder that even the loftiest dreams could be reached; it was a stepping stone on her journey to unravel the universe's secrets.

Aoife knew her path wouldn't be easy. Leaving Ballymuckmore, defying expectations, meant leaving behind everything she knew. But as she stood in the cold autumn air, her shiny new telescope pointed towards the star-dusted sky, she felt a newfound resolve. The whispers of the stars were louder now, urging her onward. She was Aoife, the girl who dreamt of stars, and no matter the obstacles, she wouldn't let anyone dim her stardust dreams. And under the watchful gaze of the universe, she took her first step, not towards the distant galaxies, but towards the courage to chase them, one starlit night at a time.

Push Comes to Shove

Sheebie stretched out her tape measure across the width of the engine and made a note of the measurement. Then she took down the measurement of its length. She then repeated the exercise just to make sure.
"Yup," she declared.
The magnificent engine, Aoife's crowning achievement, gleamed in the still's firelight, an undeniable testament to her ingenuity.
"The doors too small. How are we getting that monster out of here?" Sheebie's voice echoed the unspoken concern in everyone's eyes.
They all stared at it, the doorway, narrow and unassuming, suddenly seemed as imposing as a standing stone.
The group fell silent, a tableau of furrowed brows and gnawed fingernails. Finny, usually the optimist, scratched his head, his whistle dwindling to a sheepish cough. Even Aoife, the rocket engine queen herself, had a hint of worry creasing her forehead.
"Well," Leaky finally broke the silence, his voice raspy like the sound of a potato stuck in a grater, "if the door ain't big enough, make a bigger one, right?"
Heads swivelled towards him. Leaky, the resident tinkerer, his mind as cluttered as his shed, often came up with the simplest, yet most outrageous solutions.
"A bigger door?" Finny echoed, skeptical, yet intrigued.
Leaky grinned, his teeth as yellow as a sun-soaked potato.
"Aye, lad," he drawled, pointing to the wall beside the existing entrance. "We build a double door, like a giant trap. One big door slides open wide, and in it, a smaller one like a hatch on a

leprechaun's breeches. The small one lets us out and the big one lets us waltz the engine out whenever we need to."
Aoife considered it, her eyes sparkling with the thrill of a new challenge. "It'll work," she mused, tracing the outline of the proposed doors with her fingers. "We could even build tracks, like those used for peat barges, to slide the big door on."
Finny rubbed his chin, picturing the scene. "And make it open with a lever," he added, his voice brimming with excitement, "like something out of a pirate ship!"
Ideas began to snowball, one topping the last. They envisioned pulleys and winches, ramps and rollers, all powered by the magic of potcheen fuelled ingenuity. Leaky, his eyes twinkling like bits of broken glass in the firelight, sketched furiously on a scrap of paper, his drawings resembling a potato's fever dream. As the moon climbed higher, bathing the shed in its silvery glow, they worked, sustained by mugs of potato hooch and dreams as boundless as the sky. The impossible task of removing the engine transformed into a joyous game, a testament to their collective madness and unwavering belief in their collective power.
The shed, once a chaotic haven of mismatched tools and half-finished contraptions, had become a workshop of dreams, humming with the promise of grand escapes and potato-powered revolutions. The engine, still nestled within, but with a path to freedom now visible, seemed to sigh in anticipation, its metallic heart echoing the collective pulse of the team.
The door, not just a simple exit, but a symbol of their unyielding spirit. It was be a portal, a gateway to the skies, a testament to the fact that even in the boggiest corners of Ireland, where dreams were measured in potato bushels and laughter echoed across moonlit fields, anything was possible,

as long as there was a spark of lunacy and a Ballymuckmore sized heart.

Constable O'Toole, a man built like a sturdy oak tree, squinted as the behemoth was maneuvered onto the back of his Garda truck. The "new door" Leaky had fashioned was more like a gaping maw carved into the shed wall, capable of swallowing a leprechaun's caravan whole. The potcheen engine, gleaming under the morning sun, seemed to grin back, its copper pipes glinting like mischievous eyes and its bell nozzle anticipating being rung for the first time.

"Now I've seen me share of strange contraptions in this job," O'Toole rumbled, his voice as deep as the bog at midnight, "but this, lads, takes the biscuit." He tapped the rocket nozzle and it responded with a soft note. "Ah, the nuns of the apocalypse." Finny, his chest puffed with Ballymuckmore pride, patted the engine affectionately. "Just wait till you see it roar, Constable," he boasted. "Zorg's Zenith is about to take this village to the heavens!"

Aoife chimed in with a touch of caution. "First, we need to test it," she said, her eyes sparkling with the thrill of experimentation. "The barn's all set up, and hopefully, Zorg's Zenith will prove he's worthy of a celestial tango."

The barn, an old stone structure tucked deep on the boggy extreme of Ballymuckmore, had been transformed into a test lab worthy of Zorg himself. Aoife, with Leaky's help, had built a sturdy rig, anchoring the engine to the earth while allowing it to unleash its potcheen fury. Cables snaked out like potato vines, sensors and gauges blinking like fireflies caught in a jar. The tension in the air was thicker than potato stew. Even Constable O'Toole, usually unflappable, shifted his weight nervously. This was it, the moment of truth. Would Zorg's

Zenith live up to the hype, or would it splutter and cough like a potato past its prime?

Aoife, her fingers hovering over the control panel, took a deep breath. "Ready?" she asked, her voice barely a whisper.

Finny squeezed her hand, his eyes mirroring her own anxious excitement. "Ready as we'll ever be, spud-scientist," he replied. With a flick of a switch, a spark of electricity coursed through the engine.

The fuel ignited with a series of pops and sputters, each one chiming against the engine nozzle with a different note. As the engine grew louder, the chimes combined into a beautiful symphony that echoed across the bog. It was the voice of Spudnik.

The ground trembled, the barn walls shook, and the engine, bathed in a blue fiery glow, seemed to dance with manic joy. Gauges flickered, needles pirouetted, and a plume of potato-scented smoke filled the air. The test rig creaked under the strain, but held firm. Then, a joyous shout rang out: "We have thrust! It's working!"

Aoife, tears of relief and elation mingling with the soot on her cheeks, pumped her fist in the air. Finny whooped with delight, throwing his arms around her. Even Constable O'Toole, a man not prone to displays of emotion, managed a rare, potato-shaped grin.

The test wasn't perfect. The engine sputtered and hiccuped, a temperamental beast still learning to harness its new power. But it worked. It pushed, it roared, it promised the impossible. In that dusty barn, amongst the smell of burnt potatoes and the symphony of whirring gears, Ballymuckmore's dream of celestial flight had taken its first wobbly step.

The journey ahead was long and uncertain, filled with all manner of hurdles and cosmic curves. But as they watched the engine cool, its fiery heart still glowing with the echo of its first celestial dance, one thing was clear: Ballymuckmore, armed with Zorg's Zenith and driven by dreams bigger than its bog, was ready to reach for the stars. The stars, it seemed, weren't just twinkling in the night sky; they were inviting Spudnik to come and dance with them across the inky blackness.

Rattlin' Bog

Wednesday nights in Ballymuckmore thrummed with a different kind of energy. The air itself vibrated with anticipation, a melody waiting to be played. Forget the usual peat smoke and murmur of gossip in the Pub with No Name; this was the night for music, for laughter, for the very soul of Ballymuckmore to pour forth in a symphony of mismatched instruments and heartfelt song. A joyous cacophony of a community in harmony.
As dusk settled, casting long shadows across the bog, instruments emerged from dusty corners and hidden compartments. Finny, ever the enthusiast, arrived first, his battered banjo slung across his back, an excited glint in his eye. Soon, others followed. Aoife, her hair ablaze in the firelight, cradled her fiddle close and Sheebie settled in with her well loved flute case.
Agnes, the pub's ever-gracious owner, surveyed the scene with a twinkle in her eye. She bustled about, replenishing pints and pouring generous measures of potcheen and setting out plates laden with her legendary soda bread. The pub filled with the warmth of bodies and the murmur of excited greetings.
"Are yer well, Sheebie? Ready to avoid a repeat of last week's 'Samba' incident?" Finny winked as he made a last minute adjustment of his banjo strings.
Sheebie, her brow furrowed in concentration as she assembled her flute, glanced up with a deadpan expression. "Finny, for the last time, there was no 'incident.' It was merely a… creative interpretation of the rhythm."
Finny chuckled, the sound warm and familiar. "Creative indeed, especially when it involved you launching into a jig while the rest of us were playing a mournful ballad."

Sheebie rolled her eyes playfully. "Artistic license, Finny. Besides, who says a spud can't have a jig in its heart?"
Finny grinned. "Fair enough. But tonight, let's try to keep the spud-jigging to a minimum, alright? Agnes might start withholding the potcheen if she thinks the music's gonna give her a heart attack again."
Sheebie snorted. "As if Agnes would deny anyone potcheen, especially on music night. But fine, I'll try to resist the urge to break into a spontaneous jig... unless, of course, the spirit moves me."
"The spirit, or the potcheen?" Finny teased, winking.
Sheebie strummed a chord, a mischievous glint forever in her eyes. "Let's just say the two often have a... close working relationship."
Finny threw his head back and laughed, the sound echoing through the cozy pub. "Alright, you win. Just promise me, no rogue jigs tonight. "
Sheebie smirked. "No promises, Finny. But hey, if the music takes us there, who are we to argue with the spud-powered muse?"
"Where's Leaky?" Aoife asked as she scanned the door. "He wouldn't miss music night for the world, not even for potcheen."
Suddenly, the door burst open with a bang. Leaky, eyes wide and panting like a dog who'd chased a runaway spud, tumbled into the pub.
The conversations faltered, replaced by murmurs of curiosity as Leaky made his way deliberately across the room, towards his usual seat. The Constable, ever the stoic observer, raised a single eyebrow. "Something different about you tonight, Lad," he drawled, "but I can't quite put my finger on it..."

"Have you had a hair cut.... or maybe trimmed your beard?" Sheebie inquired, her straight face straining to contain her amusement.

Leaky puffed out his chest, preparing his grand reveal, but Finny, never one to miss a beat, let out a snort. "Is that… a new after shave you're wearing?"

The room chuckled, but Leaky remained undeterred. He threw back his head, ready to explain what everyone could plainly see, when Sheebie's sharp eyes landed on the glinting object he had on his hip.

"By the saints," she gasped, "is that a… sword?"

The collective chuckle morphed into stunned silence. Leaky, seeing the direction their attention had taken, beamed and whipped the sword from its sheath.

"Behold!" he declared, striking a dramatic pose, "I am Leakius Maximus, Spud Conqueror of all Ballymuckmore!"

He stood tall and proud, adorned in a full Roman centurion's ensemble, complete with a gleaming bronze breastplate, sturdy leather sandals, and a skirt that flirted with the knobbliest knees this side of Kilcorney. The plume atop his helmet danced in the flickering lights of the bar, a beacon of ancient glory amidst the modern revelry.

Finny slid a pint of Guinness in front of his friend as Leaky took his seat. "Washing machine playing up again?"

Leaky just nodded, picked up his pint and took a long steady drink.

Feeling suitably refreshed, he pulled out a battered tin whistle, his eyes twinkling, and played a quick series of notes, as if summoning an Oompa Loompa.

"Alright, let's get this music night started! Who's ready for some banging tunes and Leaky's legendary whistle-juggling?"

Finny grinned, banjo poised. "Now you're talking, Leakius! Let's show the spuds what Ballymuckmore session night is all about!"

The music began tentatively, a single fiddle note followed by the soft strum of a guitar. Then, as if cued by an invisible conductor, the pub erupted in a symphony of sound. Finny's banjo launched into a lively jig, his voice booming with gusto. Aoife's fiddle soared, its melody weaving through the air like a playful wisp of smoke. Constable O'Toole's guitar added a melancholic counterpoint, a bittersweet undercurrent to the joyful din.

Soon, the pub was alive with sound. Villagers young and old joined in, some with instruments, others with voices raised in song. Traditional jigs mingled with contemporary tunes, laughter punctuated the melodies, and feet tapped to the infectious rhythm. There was Michael Flatley, his tanned face creased in a smile as he played the spoons with surprising dexterity whilst his feet seem to have an energy all of their own.

An old villager in the corner, eyes closed, swaying, his leathery hands tapping out a silent rhythm on his knee. A young girl, perched on a stool beside her grandmother, sang along with surprising gusto, with a voice as pure as the mountain air, her eyes shining with the innocent joy of discovery. Even the ever-grumpy spinster Maguire, notorious for her sharp tongue, couldn't resist the pull of the music, her lips twitching into a reluctant smile.

Agnes, the pub's ever-present matriarch, surveyed the scene with a contented smile. Her face crinkled with amusement as Constable O'Toole, usually so serious in his Garda uniform, attempted a jig, his two left feet somehow adding to the merriment. Beside him, Laoise, her golden hair shining in the firelight, belted out a bawdy ballad with gusto, her voice as strong and vibrant as the potcheen she was consuming.

The music wasn't polished, not perfect. Notes were missed, voices cracked, and the occasional errant spoon clattered to the floor. But the imperfections only added to the charm, each fumble a testament to the shared spirit of the moment. Young and old, newcomer and lifelong resident, all joined in the joyous cacophony, their voices blending in a chorus of community and belonging.

When the last note faded, a comfortable silence descended, thick with unspoken emotions. Then, a smattering of applause broke the quiet, soon swelling into a wave of appreciation that washed over the makeshift band. Faces glowed in the firelight, eyes shining with the warmth of shared experience.

"Another Wednesday well spent," Seamus declared, wiping sweat from his brow with a laugh.

"Indeed," Laoise agreed, her voice husky from singing. "Until next week, Ballymuckmore!"

The chorus of "Aye!" that echoed through the pub was more than just agreement; it was a promise, a reaffirmation of the bonds that tied them together. In the Pub with No Name, on Wednesday nights, the music wasn't just entertainment; it was the heartbeat of the village, a celebration of their differences and their shared humanity, a testament to the enduring power of community, spun from laughter, music, and the occasional rogue spoon. As they drifted out into the starlit night, the melody of their shared joy lingered in the air, a reminder that even in a village as quirky as Ballymuckmore, the truest music was always played together.

The raucous laughter of Agnes' Pub faded behind them, replaced by the gentle murmur of the moonlit night. Finny, Aoife, and Sheebie walked shoulder-to-shoulder, their steps

light with the shared merriment of the evening. Their guide wasn't the usual moonlight, but the lilting melody of "The Rattlin' Bog" escaping Centurion Leakius' tin whistle.
As the tune filled Finny's head, new lyrics emerged. He started singing.

"Rare bog, a rattlin' bog, a bog down in the valley-o.
Rare bog, a rattlin' bog, a bog down in the valley-o"
On that bog there stands a launchpad.
Rare launchpad, a rattlin' launchpad.
Launchpad on the bog. "

Aoife and Sheebie joined in.
"And the bog down in the valley-o.
Rare bog, a rattlin' bog, a bog down in the valley-o.
Rare bog, a rattlin' bog, a bog down in the valley-o"

Sheebie took the lead.
"On that launchpad there was a Rocket.
Rare Rocket, a rattlin' rocket.
Rocket on the Launchpad"

They all joined in
"Launchpad on the bog.
Rare bog, a rattlin' bog, a bog down in the valley-o.
Rare bog, a rattlin' bog, a bog down in the valley-o"

Aoife took her turn "On that Rocket there was a engine. Rare engine, a rattlin's engine. Engine on the rocket"

"Rocket on the Launchpad .
Launchpad on the bog.

Rare bog, a rattlin' bog, a bog down in the valley-o.
Rare bog, a rattlin' bog, a bog down in the valley-o"

The verses continued down the cobbled street becoming more absurd the further they got from the pub.

For the discerning reader, you may have noticed that in the enchanted realm of Ballymuckmore, the sun is always shining, and evenings are adorned with moonbeams and stardust. While it's true that rain is a frequent visitor in Ireland, poetic license granted me the liberty to omit those dreary and dismal days from our tale. And yes, in reality, this adventure did take an exceedingly long time to unfold – but like a fine potcheen (if there is such a thing) or a well-aged cheese, some things are worth the wait.

Alien Encounters

The blue glow, a daily beacon in the boggy dawn, as Aoife continued her engine testing had become a ticking potato bomb, attracting more than just moths and curious sheep. The tin-foil brigade, their antennas twitching with renewed fervour, descended on Ballymuckmore like a flock of birds to a newly cleaned car. Armed with theories wilder than a leprechaun on moonshine, they interrogated Agnes in her pub, their questions bouncing off the walls like rogue potatoes.
"Blue glow in the bog, woman!" one squinty-eyed man, his hat adorned with a satellite dish, jabbed a finger at Agnes. "Aliens? Leprechauns gone rogue?"
Agnes snorted into her mug of tea. "Aliens? In Ballymuckmore? More likely the bog lights, green as a shamrock and just as mischievous. Or maybe," she winked, her eyes twinkling like fairy lights, "the little people of the bog, having a moonlit rave with potato hooch."
The tin-foil brigade, baffled by Agnes's nonchalance, huddled together, their whispers buzzing like bees around a honeypot. The blue glow, shrouded in Agnes's cryptic words, became a Rorschach test for conspiracy theories. Some saw alien spaceships, others secret government experiments, and a few, kindled by Agnes's suggestion, even envisioned dancing leprechauns with glowing lanterns.
The village, already buzzing with the anticipation of the Beautiful Ireland competition, erupted in a cacophony of speculation. The rumours spread like wildfire, encouraged by Agnes's sly asides and Leaky's embellished tales of Zorg and his Zenith. Tourists, seeking the thrill of the unknown, mingled with the tin-foil brigade, their cameras hungry for the next Ballymuckmore sensation.

Finny and Aoife, torn between amusement and concern, watched the madness unfold. Their precious Spudnik engine, hidden in a barn on the bog , was now the subject of outlandish theories and tabloid headlines. Should they reveal the truth, risking ridicule and jeopardising their competition hopes? Or should they let the rumours simmer, a pot of lunacy bubbling away, adding to the village's chaotic charm?

As the sun dipped below the bog, casting long shadows over the thatched roofs, Ballymuckmore found itself at a crossroads. The blue glow, a mere byproduct of Zorg's Zenith, had become a catalyst, igniting a whirlwind of speculation and transforming the village into a stage for a cosmic farce. The question wasn't just about aliens and leprechaun raves; it was about the power of stories, the beauty of lunacy, and the delicate dance between truth and fantasies that made Ballymuckmore, well, Ballymuckmore.

Aoife, her brow furrowed like a potato field in a drought, surveyed the chaos. The village, usually a symphony of sheep bleats and Agnes's hearty laughter, was now a cacophony of whispers and wild theories. The tin-foil brigade, their hats bristling with antennae, stalked the bog like extraterrestrial bloodhounds, their eyes fixed for the phantom blue glow.

"We can't let these rumours spiral out of control," Aoife declared, her voice firm as a cobblestone path. "But we also can't reveal Spudnik just yet. We need... a diversion."

Finny, his brow furrowed in thought, scratched his chin, the sound like a finger nail against a cheese grater. "A diversion, you say? One that's both believable and... potato-powered?"

A mischievous glint flickered in Aoife's eyes. "Precisely," she said, a smile spreading across her face like butter on a hot scone. "Remember those bog gases Leaky was talking about? The ones that glow blue when ignited?"

Finny's eyes widened, the cogs whirring in his head. "So you're saying…?"

"We create another blue glow, well away from the village" Aoife grinned, her voice dropping to a conspiratorial whisper. "A permanent one, fuelled by the bog itself, a perpetual beacon to distract the theorists and keep our secrets safe."

The plan was audacious, a MacGyver masterpiece. Aoife, armed with Leaky's rusty tools and Finny's unwavering optimism, ventured deep into the bog, following the secret paths known only to the village elders and the sly foxes. They laid pipes, and rigged up a contraption that looked like a cross between a moonshine still and a leprechaun's teapot.

The heart of the operation was a copper nozzle, polished to a gleam that rivalled the moon itself. Aoife, her fingers nimble as a potato peeler, crafted it with meticulous care, channeling the bog gases through its narrow opening. One spark, and the nozzle would become a celestial flamethrower, painting the night sky with a permanent blue glow.

As the moon climbed, casting long shadows across the bog, Aoife and Finny, weary but triumphant, ignited the contraption. A soft hiss, a crackle of flame, and then… a dazzling blue light erupted from the nozzle, bathing the bog in an otherworldly glow. It pulsed and danced, a mesmerising beacon in the night, a testament to Ballymuckmore's lunacy and Aoife's scientific brilliance.

Aoife and Finny, their faces lit by the celestial blue, exchanged a smile. They had bought themselves time, a buffer between their Spudnik and the prying eyes of the world. The blue glow, a shimmering secret in the bog, was more than just a diversion; it was a symbol of their village's spirit, a testament to their ability to dream bigger than their bog, their flames burning bright in the face of lunacy and laughter.

And as the first rays of dawn kissed the bog, painting the blue light with a new hue, one thing was certain: Ballymuckmore, the village that dared to dream with potatoes and moonshine, had just added another layer of lunacy to its already chaotic charm.

The tin-foil brigade, drawn like moths to a flame, descended upon the spectacle. Theories flew faster than a sheepdog chasing a rogue potato. Were they witnessing an alien landing site? A portal to another dimension? Or, as Agnes, ever the joker, quipped, "just the bog people playing tricks on ya, lads.", which was closer to the truth than she realised.

The village, caught between amusement and awe, watched the blue glow, mesmerised. Ballymuckmore, once a sleepy village, was now a stage for a cosmic spectacle, fed by bog gases and potato-powered ingenuity. The rumours, though wilder than ever, had taken a new turn, a whimsical twist that only Ballymuckmore could pull off.

Operation Spudzilla

Ballymuckmore was in a state of glorious pandemonium. Between the Beautiful Ireland competition, the ufologists buzzing over the blue glow like wasps around a jam jar, and now a RTE camera crew descended upon the village like a flock of starlings, it was enough to make Finny forget what day of the week it was. He knew it wasn't Saturday because he'd not had breakfast.
The camera crew, armed with microphones and questions sharper than Leaky's rusty tools, interviewed the villagers, their every answer adding fuel to the fire of speculation. Sheebie, ever the pragmatic voice, stuck to bog gas explanations, her skepticism echoing the bleats of the confused sheep. Agnes, however, gleefully sprinkled the story with tales of dancing leprechauns and potato moonshine, leaving the camera crew with eyes as wide as saucers and notebooks filled with lunacy.
Finny and Aoife, their smiles strained under the glare of the spotlight, tried to steer the conversation towards the Beautiful Ireland competition. They spoke of their hanging flower baskets, their potato-powered irrigation system, and their plans for a potato themed tea room. But the camera crew, their eyes glued to the blue glow in the distance, seemed more interested in extraterrestrial visitors than hanging petunias.
Their plan to divert attention away from the village had backfired, majorly.
The village, usually buzzing with the cheerful chaos of everyday life, became a stage for an unintentional documentary. Tourists jostled with ufologists, their cameras clicking and whispers buzzing like a swarm of potato flies. Agnes's pub overflowed with thirsty reporters and bewildered

locals, the air thick with the smell of proper Irish hooch and outrageous theories.

Ballymuckmore's carefully crafted plans for the Beautiful Ireland competition lay trampled under the hooves of this unexpected stampede. Their beautiful hanging baskets remained unhung, the potato irrigation system lay forgotten in the shed, and the potato themed tea room remained a figment of Finny's vivid imagination.

As the RTE cameras rolled, capturing the village's lunacy in all its glory, Aoife and Finny exchanged a worried look. Their little secret, Zorg's Zenith nestled in Leaky's shed, seemed precariously close to exposure. The potato-powered rocket, once a whimsical dream, now felt like a ticking time bomb, one that could explode their plans for the competition and launch them into the stratosphere of national ridicule.

The blue glow, a luminous symbol of their ingenuity, hung over the village like a mocking moon. It had drawn the crowds, ignited the theories, and threatened to derail their dreams. Yet, amidst the chaos, there was a spark of defiance in Ballymuckmore's eyes. This wasn't just about a competition; it was about their village, their lunacy, and their combined spirit. They couldn't stop the cameras, the tourists, or the conspiracy theories. But they could, they would, show the world the true beauty of Ballymuckmore. Perhaps, their competition entry wouldn't be hanging baskets and tea rooms. Perhaps, it would be a documentary of sorts, a wild, potato-powered ride through their bog-drenched village, highlighted by lunacy and laughter, with a blue glow in the sky as their crowning glory.

Sheebie, her brow, a furrowed one more like a freshly tilled potato field, the perpetual mischievous glint in her eye. "Why attract the attention to Ballymuckmore?" she asked, a smile tugging at the corner of her lips. "Let's give those Kilmuckety lads a taste of their own medicine."

The Spudnik team, huddled over Agnes's best potato bread (though Finny swore he heard Agnes mutter something about "potato-brained ideas" under her breath), considered Sheebie's plan. It was audacious, a touch devious, and, dare they say, delightfully potato-powered.

Their target: Kilmuckety, the neighbouring village, always eager to steal Ballymuckmore's thunder (and possibly Agnes's award-winning potato recipes). The plan? To create a spectacle so bizarre, so utterly confounding, that it would lure every camera crew, UFO enthusiast, and spuddle-brained tourist away from Ballymuckmore and towards Kilmuckety's unsuspecting valley.

Finny, his imagination always benefitted from a good potato pancake, envisioned flashing lights, unearthly sounds, maybe even a giant inflatable spud bouncing across the Kilmuckety hills. Aoife, ever the scientist, cautioned against anything too outlandish, suggesting strategically placed mirrors and controlled methane releases to create a convincing aurora borealis effect.

"And what about Agnes?" Leaky scratched his head, his face crinkling in concern. "The pub's busier than a spud harvest with all these visitors. Moving them won't be easy, even with the best Irish hooch."

Sheebie winked. "Leave that to me," she said, a sly grin playing on her lips. "I have a few… persuasive arguments planned for those glued to Agnes's bar stools." Sheebie, it seemed, had her own brand of charm, a blend of wit and practicality that could lure even the most stubborn away from a warm mug.

The plan took shape, helped by late-night potcheen powered brainstorming sessions, and a healthy dose of laughter. Leaky, with his toolbox overflowing with repurposed contraptions, would work on the lights and sounds. Aoife, armed with scientific formulas and Leaky's questionable engineering, would orchestrate the "aurora borealis." And Finny, his imagination running wild, would be in charge of the "giant inflatable spud"

As for Sheebie, well, she had her own methods. Whispers of complimentary pints at a mysterious "speakeasy" in Kilmuckety, rumours of a leprechaun treasure hunt hidden in the bog, and perhaps a well-placed "systems malfunction" at the pub - all carefully orchestrated to lead the unsuspecting tourists and reporters astray.

The operation, dubbed "Operation Spudzilla," was risky, a chaotic dance on the edge of lunacy. But for the Spudnik team, it was the only way to ensure their precious rocket's safety. Ballymuckmore might lose the Beautiful Ireland competition, but they would gain something far more valuable: the freedom to launch Spudnik on their own terms.

As the moon cast its silvery glow over the bog, the Spudnik team with the help of a handful of villagers, set their plan in motion. Kilmuckety, unsuspecting and blissfully unaware, was about to experience a night it wouldn't soon forget. The village of Ballymuckmore, cloaked in a veil of secrecy and laughter, held its breath, ready to watch their audacious plan unfold. This wasn't just about Spudnik; it was about proving that even a small village, armed with lunacy and a whole lot of spirit, could outwit its rivals and create a spectacle that would forever be etched in the annals of Irish lore.

The night promised to be one of epic proportions, a testament to Ballymuckmore's spirit, a cosmic caper fuelled by dreams, laughter, and a huge heart. And as the last glimmer of the sun disappeared over the horizon, one thing was certain: Ballymuckmore, the village that dared to dream with potatoes and moonshine, was never going to be boring. They were off to the races, not just towards the stars, but towards a potato-powered victory of a different kind, leaving behind a trail of laughter, lunacy, and a bewildered Kilmuckety in their wake. The night sky, usually a tapestry of twinkling stars, was tonight marred by the sickly green glow emanating from Kilmuckety. Operation Spudzilla, Ballymuckmore's potato-powered symphony of confusion, was in full swing. Leaky, his face illuminated by the flickering disco lights, wrestled with the washing machine motor, coaxing it into a semblance of extraterrestrial hum.

Finny, perched on the tractor roof, wrestled with a different kind of beast: Spudzilla, the inflating monstrosity, seemed determined to remain stubbornly grounded.

Aoife was stunned. "What are you doing with a giant inflatable spud? When you said a 'Giant inflatable spud' I didn't think you meant a 'Giant inflatable spud' "

"Er, I acquired it a few years ago after the Count Cork Fair. Thought it might come in handy someday."

Aoife just shook her head and watched as the 'Murphy's Spuds' balloon slowly took shape.

"More helium!" Finny bellowed, his voice muffled by the potato nose he'd insisted on wearing as a disguise (much to Aoife's amusement). Sheebie, flitting through the shadows like a mischievous leprechaun, dodged stray potato tendrils and muttered reassurances. "Patience, Finny! Spudzilla will fly, even if it takes all the spuds in Ballymuckmore!"

Agnes, lured from the pub by the promise of "potato-powered fireworks" (Leaky's euphemism for the methane vents), surveyed the scene with a critical eye. "Not bad, lads," she grunted, adjusting her floral-print beret. "But where's the spud in this spud show? Needs more sparkle, more… potatoey pizazz!"

As if on cue, the washing machine motor sputtered and died, spewing a plume of smoke that temporarily obscured Spudzilla from view. Panic surged through the team like a rogue spud in a stew pot. Leaky sputtered technobabble about faulty relays and capacitor overload, while Finny battled a rising tide of helium-induced hiccups.

Suddenly, a gust of wind, mischievous and opportune, caught Spudzilla's bulbous form. With a groan that could have been classified as bovine, celestial or Finny after a hearty breakfast, the giant spud waddled into the air, its Christmas light eyes blinking in surprise. The cheers of the team were drowned out by the sputter of the resuscitated washing machine motor, which, in its newfound fervour, propelled Spudzilla not horizontally across the sky, but vertically.

Spudzilla, a blimp possessed by the jitters, bounced like a demented kangaroo on a pogo stick. Its eyes blinked erratically, one stuck on green, the other flashing a frantic red. The potato wings, meant for graceful gliding, flapped like a chicken in a whirlwind, offering little purchase against the night wind.

Below, the team watched in a mixture of horror and amusement as their potato-powered dreams took a decidedly un-spudlike trajectory. Agnes, sighed. "Well, lads," she said, her voice laced with a hint of begrudging admiration, "that's one way to steal the show from Kilmuckety. Though I wouldn't call it beautiful."

Sheebie, ever the optimist, saw opportunity in chaos. "Look at it, lads! Spudzilla, the dancing spud of doom! They'll never forget this in Kilmuckety, not in a million years!"
Finny, his hiccups forgotten, let out a whoop of laughter. "Spudzilla the ballerina! Spudzilla the celestial pogo stick! This is better than any speakeasy!"
Spudzilla, finally tiring of its aerial antics, descended with a graceful (well, sort of graceful) plop into a field of cabbages. The team, breathless and exhilarated, gathered around their deflated star.
Operation Spudzilla, though not the celestial ballet they'd envisioned, had achieved its mission. Kilmuckety was abuzz with tales of the dancing spud, the green lights in the sky, and the mysterious figures lurking in the shadows. The tourists and reporters, drawn by the spectacle, had abandoned Ballymuckmore, leaving Spudnik safe and sound in its Leaky-rigged haven.
Ballymuckmore, battered but not bruised, stood united in the wreckage of their potato-powered plan. They had embraced the chaos, the laughter, and the sheer audacity of their attempt, proving that even the most disastrous plans could create a spectacle that would forever be etched in the memory of their bog-soaked village.
As they surveyed the wreckage, potato by potato, one thing was certain: Ballymuckmore wouldn't be deterred. They had tasted the sweet nectar of chaos, the intoxicating aroma of lunacy, and they were hungry for more. The success of Operation Spudzilla, however accidental, had instilled in them a newfound confidence, and fresh defiance.
Aoife, rolled her eyes with a smile. "Sheebie, you and Agnes round up the stragglers and make sure everyone's got a good

breakfast. We've got a lot of work to do, and it all starts with a full belly."

Agnes, ever the queen of the pub, grinned. "Spud pancakes with extra sausages, coming right up! And for Finny, a double helping of farls, to keep him dreaming of celestial potatoes."

As dawn broke over the bog, casting long shadows across the cabbage field. Ballymuckmore buzzed with renewed energy. Spudzilla was collected from its resting place, removing any evidence of Ballymuckmores involvement in the previous night's events.

The villagers, armed with tools and good humour, began the process of resurrection. Ballymuckmore, for the first time in what seemed an age, was silent. Tranquility had returned to this oasis in the bog. The village would once again shine, ready for the Beautiful Ireland competition, one flower bed at a time.

Satin Skies

The dust of Operation Spudzilla slowly settled, leaving Ballymuckmore bathed in an unwonted silence. The tourists, once lured by the celestial caper, had vanished, leaving behind echoes of laughter and a village spick-and-span like a freshly turned potato field. Houses bore a coat of paint they hadn't seen in years, gardens teemed with new blooms, and a sense of quiet satisfaction hung in the air, thick enough to slice with a shillelagh.

But beneath the surface, a different kind of energy pulsated. In Bonanza, under the watchful eyes of Aoife and Finny, Spudnik, the potato-powered dream, neared completion. Its gleaming metal shell, cobbled together from scavenged treasures and fuelled by countless mugs of Leaky's special "rocket fuel" tea, whispered of orbital possibilities.

The only question that remained, a conundrum worthy of a leprechaun's riddle, was what colour to paint this spud-shaped envoy to the stars. Should it wear the emerald green of Ireland's rolling hills, a tribute to their bog-soaked heritage? Or perhaps the fiery orange of a sunset over Spudnik Hill, a blaze of passion against the velvet sky?

Debate raged, as passionate as a hurling match on Paddy's Day. Aoife argued for blue, mimicking the celestial exhaust trail Spudnik would undoubtedly leave in its wake. Finny, ever the dreamer, championed white, the classic colour of rockets soaring towards the cosmic unknown.

But then, in true Ballymuckmore fashion, fate intervened. A tip, whispered like a secret recipe at Agnes's pub, led them to Biddy O'Rourke's hidden paint stash. Biddy, one of the village eccentrics with a penchant for hoarding oddities, had amassed a collection of paints said to be more colourful than a field of wildflowers after a shower.

The team wasted no time and made their way to Biddy's shed, the discussion focussing on colour preferences.

"Whatever we find will have to do." Finny pointed out as they reached the shed, "we've borrowed everything else to build Spudnik. Worst case, we'll mix it all together"

Aoife turned up her nose, "Yuk! That's it, Finny no longer has any vote in what colour we paint Spudnik."

Sheebie giggled as she pulled the door open. Inside was a lifetime of questionable decorating choices, tins stacked as high as the roof.

There, amongst the dusty cans and forgotten brushes, in the far corner, was a huge plastic barrel. The side clearly labelled as paint. The budding Picassos stared at the container, whatever the colour there should be enough there to get the job done.

Aoife whispered under her breath "be blue, be blue", her fingers tightly crossed.

Finny gently wiped the dust from the lid of the barrel and laughed.

"What is, what is it ?" Aoife clamoured.

"It's not blue" Finny was trying very hard to keep a straight face.

"It's ……Satin Butterscotch".

Aoife was a bit disappointed. Leaky looked at the barrel in silence and Sheebie was laughing so much she was having difficulty catching her breath.

"Butterscotch. Not just Butterscotch, but Satin Butterscotch." Sheebie stared at the others in disbelief. "What in the name of Saint Bridget is Biddy doing with a hundred and fifty litres of Satin Butterscotch paint?"

Biddy had wanted to order a sample pot as she was thinking of painting her kitchen. Unfortunately, she got confused with litres and milli-litres and was too embarrassed to send it back. The hue, a warm golden caramel, shimmered like sun on a freshly baked potato scone. It wasn't green, or blue, or white, but it was Ballymuckmore.

It was the colour of a moonlit bog, of Agnes's legendary potato pie crust, of Finny's wildest dreams. It was unique, audacious, and utterly potato-worthy.

And so, away from curious eyes and with the bleating of sheep as background music, Spudnik was to received its final coat. Satin Butterscotch, a colour as unexpected as a leprechaun with a polka-dotted hat, adorned the potato rocket, a testament to Ballymuckmore's lunacy and their unwavering spirit.

Painting a 60-foot rocket, especially under the unorthodox guidance of the Ballymuckmore spudonauts, was guaranteed to be anything but simple. It was a recipe for glorious, potcheen powered chaos, a chance for lunacy to blossom like a rogue spud in a moonlit field.

First, there was the sheer scale of the beast. Spudnik, a spud-shaped monument to their dreams, loomed large inside Bonanza like a celestial potato ready for harvest. Reaching the upper reaches felt like scaling Mount Spudmore, requiring ladders that seemed more suited to beanstalks than potato rockets. Finny, armed with a paintbrush the size of a potato masher and boundless enthusiasm, volunteered for the summit, his ascent punctuated by vertigo-inducing whistles and near-misses with the odd startled pigeon.

Aoife took charge of the planning. She mapped out the painting process with the precision of a lunar landing, dividing the rocket into sections like a giant potato pie, assigning roles with military-like efficiency.

Like a bog flower feeling the warmth of the sun on its petals, Bonanza's roof was slowly opened. The natural light flooding in and around Spudnik as it waited for its new coat.
Leaky, meanwhile, became the resident paint chemist, concocting a unique adhesive that clung to Spudnik's metal skin like barnacles to a boat.
But Ballymuckmore wouldn't be Ballymuckmore without a healthy dose of improvised mayhem. The paint rollers, the parts scavenged from old wood sheds and rusty old washing machines, spat and sputtered like malfunctioning UFO engines, showering the team in a sticky spray of butterscotch goo. Brushes rebelled, bristles escaping in spiky protests, leading to impromptu jousting matches between Finny and Aoife (who, armed with a paintbrush the size of a broom, proved surprisingly adept at combat).
Biddy O'Rourke's Satin Butterscotch paint, initially a symbol of defiance and lunacy, turned out to be more temperamental than a leprechaun on St. Patrick's Day. The colour, originally a warm, inviting glow, took on a life of its own under Leary's imaginative interior lighting, morphing into streaks of orange, gold, and even a mischievous hint of green. Spudnik, once a sleek spud-shaped vessel, began to resemble a celestial potato kaleidoscope, a testament to Ballymuckmore's chaotic charm.
But amidst the paint splatters and potato-fuelled skirmishes, a quiet sense of accomplishment bloomed. Each brushstroke, each splatter of butterscotch, was a mark of their collective dream, a sizeable contribution to the Spudnik saga. As the sun slowly dipped below the horizon, casting long shadows on the bog, Spudnik stood sentinel, its coat of Satin Butterscotch shimmering like a cosmic spud bathed in starlight.
The painting of Spudnik may have been a chaotic caper, a ballet of mishaps and laughter. But through it all,

Ballymuckmore had once again embraced its lunacy, proving that even the simplest task, in their hands, could become a glorious spectacle, a testament to their spirit and their unwavering determination to reach for the stars, one sticky, butterscotch-streaked step at a time.

Where would Spudnik, the butterscotch rocket take them next? The answer, like the Ballymuckmore spirit itself, remained delightfully unpredictable, an open potato field of possibilities waiting to be sown.

Fun Thing, Bunting

Aoife entered the Pub with No Name like a potato-powered whirlwind, her arms laden with boxes of bunting that seemed to shimmer with a rainbow promise. In her wake followed a meticulously hand-drawn map, each cobbled street and crooked cottage marked with the precise location of its destined decoration. The village volunteers, a motley crew of enthusiasts, huddled around the map like seasoned spud farmers assessing a particularly perplexing field.
"Right lads," Aoife's voice crackled with the authority of somebody not to be messed with, "this ain't your average Sunday picnic bunting session. This is Ballymuckmore's chance to show the world we're not just a bog-soaked village with sheep problems. We're a fairy wonderland built on love, laughter, and a healthy dose of lunacy!"
The volunteers, well aware of the wrath that resided behind Aoife's kind eyes when crossed with bunting misplacement, nodded fervently. Finny, ever eager, bounced on the balls of his feet, already picturing the village transformed into a technicolor extravaganza. Sheebie, ever the pragmatist, squinted at the map, his brow furrowed like a potato field contemplating rain.
"But Aoife," he interjected, his voice carrying a hint of bog wind, "this map's more intricate than Farmer O'Malley's prize-winning parsnip maze. How are we supposed to remember which bunting goes where in this rainbow explosion?"
A mischievous glint flickered in Aoife's eyes. "Simple, Sheebie," she declared, pulling out a set of paintbrushes adorned with brightly coloured potato mashers. "Each street gets its own colour theme! Main Street will be a potato rainbow, awash in every shade of spud-skin imaginable. Down

by the bog, we'll create a field of flowers, with bunting shaped like giant potato blossoms. And Agnes's pub? Why, that'll be a giant spud pie, with bunting crust and windows sparkling like glazed berries!"

And so, the transformation began. Ballymuckmore, once a village content with its boggy charm, bloomed into a riot of colour. Bunting, like magical potato vines, clambered up cottages, draping doorways in whimsical swirls and festoons. Flower boxes overflowed with potato-themed blossoms – blooming hearts, daisies with fluffy seeds, and even a particularly audacious sunflower towering over Agnes's pub. Aoife took the opportunity to help Finny put up some of the bunting and told him stories of her life in the city before coming back to Ballymuckmore.

Finny, scratching his head with a potato-stained finger and doing his best to play the village idiot, squinted at Aoife. "So, you're tellin' me, 'cool' doesn't actually mean cold?"

Aoife, perched on a rickety ladder halfway up Ballymuckmore's newest bunting monstrosity, snorted. "Didn't I just say that, Finny? Words, they're tricky creatures, like leprechauns with a stash of riddles."

"But a spud's always cold, Aoife," Finny grumbled, his brow creased like a furrowed field. "Just like a winter bog or a sheep's nose in February."

Aoife threw him a grin, her eyes sparkling like potato-washed dewdrops. "Aye, spuds are cool like that, but 'cool' can mean other things too! Like, if you do a broom spin without falling flat on your backside, that's cool."

Finny's eyes widened like saucers. "No way! Broom spinning isn't cool, it's downright terrifying, especially after sampling Leaky's potions."

Aoife chuckled, dangling a string of rainbow bunting like a lasso. "But if you manage it without falling face-first into a mud puddle, that's pretty darn impressive, wouldn't you say?"
Finny considered this, his lips pursed as if tasting an invisible spud. "I suppose… but it still sounds dodgy. What about this 'hot' business? Is that the opposite of cool like a spud in the summer sun?"
Aoife shook her head, sending a cascade of fiery orange bunting fluttering. "Not always, Finny! Imagine Leaky's contraption finally taking flight, shooting rockets towards the moon."
Finny's jaw dropped, clattering like a loose horseshoe. "Rockets to the moon? Now that's what I call hot! Fantastically hot!"
Aoife grinned suspiciously, her eyes crinkling at the corners. "See, Finny? Words, they're like chameleons, changing colours depending on the situation. Hot can mean exciting, passionate, even spicy like Agnes's chilli sauce."
Finny scratched his chin, a thoughtful look replacing his usual spuddle-brained expression. "So, 'cool' ain't cold, and 'hot' ain't just for fires and proper mash… words are like riddles on a stick, eh?"
Aoife, the penny having finally dropped, slid gently down the ladder, and stood for a moment, staring into the depths of his blue eyes. "Eejit !"
"Some of that city stuff I really didn't know"
"Don't ya be talking to me Mr McGillicuddy" Aoife turned her stoney face away.
"But honest, Aoife.. Aoife !"
Whatever else Finny had to say was lost to Aoife as she was already half way down the cobbled street. Finny couldn't see the grin as wide as the bog stretching across her face.

The village, filled with laughter and the intoxicating scent of fresh paint, became a beehive of creativity. Finny, armed with his potato masher brush, turned lampposts into giant lollipops. Sheebie, channeling her inner leprechaun, created fairy doors woven from reeds and adorned with glistening potato pearls. Even Leaky, usually found tinkering in his shed, emerged with a contraption that sprinkled shimmering potato dust over the rooftops, creating an ethereal potato snow that glittered in the afternoon sun.

Aoife's quiet presence, flitting like a hummingbird in the bunting frenzy, was a testament to her meticulous mind. Each cobbled street, adorned with its vibrant garland, sang her silent symphony of colour and chaos. As the final bunting was secured, a sense of accomplishment settled over the village, thick and sweet like Agnes's famous potato bread.

But Aoife, ever the instigator of surprises, had one more trick up her sleeve. She summoned Finny, Sheebie, Leaky, and Zorg, their curiosity piqued by the mischievous glint in her eyes, to Mission Control, a place of whispered secrets and cables, oh so many cables.

Inside, shining like a new button, stood a contraption worthy of a leprechaun's workshop. Bunting, like a rainbow serpent, snaked its way through a side window, connecting to a large box bristling with knobs, dials, and switches. It looked like a potato-powered time machine, ready to whisk them away.

The friends, their faces etched with a mix of bewilderment and anticipation, exchanged puzzled glances. Aoife, relishing their confusion, winked with the glint of a mischief loving sprite. With a flourish, she flipped a large, chrome switch. The assembled audience held their breath.

A sign above the doorway illuminated with the word 'EXIT'.

"Wow!" Leaky could hardly contain himself.

The rest laughed as Aoife was heard muttering " Stupid wiring , agghh" while she tried to sort through a box of connectors.
"Once again" She sighed as the chrome switch was once more flipped. This time the box hummed to life. A soft whirring filled the air, as if the very fabric of the shed vibrated with anticipation.
Then, Aoife moved one of the dials, and the air crackled. A strange, distorted sound, like the laughter of a distant galaxy, filled the speakers. The friends leaned closer, their ears straining to decipher the message carried on the invisible waves.
"It's Spudnik!" Aoife exclaimed, her voice alight with potato-powered pride.
The friends looked puzzled.
"Did you not think it strange that all the bunting you've been putting up was attached to a wire? "
Finny, more confused than normal, "We just thought you'd acquired it from somewhere and anyway, it would last longer than a piece of damp string in the bog".
"No, it was deliberate. All the glorious bunting throughout the village, when connected altogether becomes the Ballymuckmore aerial. It can pick up Spudnik's signal, no matter how far it travels."
The revelation hit them like a rogue spud in a potato field. Spudnik, their celestial spud, wasn't just a one-way trip; it was a connection, a tethered thread between their village and the cosmos. They would be able to listen to its journey, its sputterings and sighs, as it danced on the edge of space.
A wave of excitement washed over them, erasing the initial confusion with a surge of potato-powered wonder. They could be there, in Mission Control, bathed in the warm glow of oil lamps and the hum of their homemade aerial, sharing in

Spudnik's adventure. They could hear its whispers from the stars, a reminder that even the most ridiculous dreams, awakened by lunacy and laughter, could reach for the cosmos. As the strange sound filled the shed, a symphony of sputters and cosmic echoes, the friends knew they were no longer just villagers. They were the spudnik team, ground control to Major Spudnik, connected by a rainbow of bunting and a shared love for the impossible. And as they listened to their celestial spud sail through the invisible waves, one thing was certain: Ballymuckmore, the village that dared to paint the cosmos with Satin Butterscotch, was on a journey that would forever etch its name in the annals of potato-powered lore.

The countdown had begun, not just for Spudnik's launch, but for a new chapter in Ballymuckmore's history. The stars, once a distant dream, were now a crackling whisper in their ears, a promise of potato-fuelled adventures yet to come. And as the moon peeked over the bog, casting a silvery glow on the village transformed, one thing was certain: Ballymuckmore was never going to be boring.

Loaves and Fishes

The crisp Sunday air held the tang of peat smoke and the promise of rain, clinging to Finny's hair like cobwebs as he walked the familiar path toward the church. His boots, caked in the rich, black mud of the bog, squelched with each step, a rhythmic counterpoint to the chatter around him.

Beside him, Sheebie shuffled along, her silence a quiet melody compared to Agnes's booming voice, already expounding on the merits of her prize-winning turnips to anyone within earshot. Leaky trailed behind, muttering to himself about the "celestial mechanics" of church bells and the possibility of harnessing their sound as an alternative potato-peeling power source.

Sheebie, letting Leaky catch her up, nudged him with her elbow. "So, Leaky, you ready for another dose of Father Dougal's ecumenical musings?"

Leaky adjusted the goggles perched atop his unruly hair. "Musings? More like ramblings, wouldn't you say, Sheebie? Though, I must admit, the man has a certain… unorthodox charm."

Sheebie chuckled, a low rumble in her chest. "Unorthodox is one way to put it. But I'm curious, Leaky, with all your theories about ley lines and alien spud farmers… do you actually believe in all that Father Dougal preaches?"

Leaky tugged at his beard, a thoughtful frown creasing his brow. "Believe? Not in the traditional sense, perhaps. But there's something about this universe, Sheebie, something beyond our spud-patch understanding. Maybe Father Dougal, with his… unique perspective, stumbles upon some truths from time to time, hidden in plain sight."

Sheebie raised an eyebrow, her lips twitching with amusement. "Hidden truths, or just a good dram of potcheen before his sermons?"

Leaky harrumphed. "Now, Sheebie, that's just slander! Though, I wouldn't blame the man for seeking some… spiritual lubrication before facing a congregation like ours." He winked at her, a glint in his eye.

Finny, walking just ahead of them, couldn't help but grin. He knew Sheebie was just poking fun, but Leaky's flustered defences were always a source of amusement.

"Speaking of lubrication," Sheebie continued, her voice dripping with mock innocence, "do you think Spudnik needs a special blessing before it takes off? Maybe some celestial WD-40 to keep those potato-powered engines purring?"

Leaky, now fully engaged, puffed out his chest. "Nonsense! Spudnik is a marvel of Ballymuckmore ingenuity, fuelled by the collective spirit of this village. No fancy blessings needed, just good elbow grease and a dash of Seamus's lucky fur!"

Sheebie burst out laughing, her eyes sparkling with their resident mischief. "Oh, Leaky, you never disappoint! Just remember, if Spudnik starts malfunctioning mid-flight, don't blame Father Dougal for neglecting his blessing duties."

Leaky shook his head, a smile tugging at his lips despite himself. "You're incorrigible, Sheebie. But I wouldn't have you any other way. Now, come on, let's get up there before Father Dougal starts his sermon on the theological implications of spud-shaped clouds."

The path wound through fields dotted with sheep, their woolly forms grazing peacefully, oblivious to the impending sermon. Finny, despite his usual irreverence, felt a familiar warmth bloom in his chest. Sundays, with their well-worn rituals and

Father Dougal's unpredictable sermons, were an anchor in the whirlwind of Ballymuckmore's lunacy.

As they neared the church, the scent of turf fire smoke mingled with the faint aroma of Mrs. O'Leary's baking, a tantalising promise of post-service spuds and gossip. The whitewashed church, crowned with a moss-covered steeple, stood watch over the village, its crooked windows reflecting the sky like mismatched eyes.

Children, their laughter echoing like wind chimes, chased each other between gravestones, their Sunday best stained green with the remnants of bog adventures. Seamus, the ever-present sheepdog, trotted alongside Sheebie, a contented glint in his eye, no doubt dreaming of pilfering sausages from unsuspecting picnickers after the service.

Reaching the churchyard, Finny fell into step with Aoife, her hair escaping its usual braid in a halo of fiery curls. "Ready for another round of Father Dougal's divine spud-ponderings?" she asked, a twinkle in her eyes.

Finny grinned. "Ready as I'll ever be, Aoife. Though, I wouldn't mind if this week's sermon stayed earthbound for a change."

They joined the throng on the steps, a kaleidoscope of mismatched hats and worn boots. As the bell clanged its final call, a hush fell over the crowd, anticipation crackling in the air. The doors creaked open, beckoning them inside, and Ballymuckmore, with its mud-caked boots and potato-powered dreams, prepared to embark on another Sunday adventure, led by a priest whose sermons were as legendary as the village itself.

Inside the stone walls of the church, a congregation of mismatched chairs creaked under the weight of anticipation. Agnes, her Sunday bonnet adorned with a suspiciously potato-shaped feather, fidgeted, eager for the priest's latest theological escapade. Seamus, the sheepdog, snuck in under a pew, hoping for a surreptitious nap amidst the sermon's inevitable tangents. Father Dougal, a man with eyebrows that seemed to permanently question the existence of scissors, strode to the pulpit. His gaze, usually lost in the contemplation of distant sheep clouds, landed on the congregation. A mischievous twinkle ignited within.

"Brothers and sisters," he began, his voice a warm rumble, "today's gospel tells the story of the loaves and fishes. Now, I've been ponderin', did Jesus ever consider spuds? Imagine the miracle – potato power, that's what I say! Imagine the multitudes fed on a mountain of fluffy mash! Would they have served baked potatoes at the last supper?"

Agnes, her eyes wide, whispered to Finny, "Do you think he'll mention the incident with the holy water and the potcheen again?" Finny shrugged, a silent prayer escaping his lips for a sermon mercifully devoid of their past embarrassments.

Undeterred, Father Dougal continued, his sermon taking unexpected detours through the history of potato farming, the theological implications of spud-shaped clouds, and a particularly heated debate with a particularly skeptical robin perched on the windowsill. The congregation, used to the priest's unique style, chuckled and nodded, their faces a tapestry of amusement and bemusement.

As the sermon drew to a close, Father Dougal, with a flourish, pulled out a small, misshapen potato. "And remember, my flock, even the smallest spud, with a little faith and a sprinkle of divine intervention, can achieve great things."

A collective sigh of relief rippled through the church. No potcheen anecdotes, no existential musings on the afterlife of sheep. Just a simple, heartfelt message delivered in true Father

Dougal fashion. As they filed out, the villagers exchanged smiles and knowing winks. Sunday service wasn't just about piety, it was about community, laughter, and the comfort of knowing that even in the grand scheme of the cosmos, Ballymuckmore, with its quirky priest and lofty dreams, held a unique and cherished place.

Leaky, beard bristling with newfound inspiration, bounced down the hill from church, trailed by an amused Finny, Sheebie, and Aoife. Still buzzing from Father Dougal's spud-tastic sermon, Leaky couldn't shake the image of Jesus multiplying spuds instead of loaves and fishes.

"Imagine if history had a potato twist!" he exclaimed, waving his arms like a windmill. "Think of the possibilities! Caesar conquering Gaul with spud-powered catapults, launching mashed potatoes instead of stones!"

Finny snorted, wiping away a tear of laughter. "You're off your rocker, Leaky. Romans would've gotten heartburn before they conquered anything."

Aoife, her eyes gleaming, added, "King Arthur and the Knights of the Round Spud! Their quest? To find the Holy Grail… filled with the most perfect potcheen in the land!"

"Now you're talking my kinda language." Leaky proclaimed. Sheebie, caught up in the spirit, couldn't help but contribute. "The Spudnish Armada! Launching a fleet of potato-shaped ships to conquer England, only to be defeated by a swarm of hungry seagulls!"

Their laughter echoed through the bog, bouncing off the ancient stones and startling a flock of sheep. As they descended, the church faded into the background, replaced by the familiar patchwork of fields and hay bales. Yet, the world around them seemed different, infused with the whimsical possibilities of a potato-powered past.

"Maybe Father Dougal's onto something," Aoife mused, wiping tears of mirth from her eyes. "Who knows what history might have been, with a touch of true Irish magic?"

City Lights

In the middle of the whirlwind of bunting, potato-powered inventions, and celestial dreams, a gentler current flowed between Aoife and Finny. Their blossoming relationship, once a quiet bud in the chaos, now yearned for sunlight. Finny, sensing this, understood that even among the unending madness of Ballymuckmore, love needed its own space to bloom.
"Aoife," he said, his voice a calm anchor among the cacophony, "all this is amazing, Spudnik and the bunting and everything. But I feel like... we haven't seen each other, not really, not for a while."
Aoife, her eyes usually sparkling with potato-powered mischief, softened. The village's transformation, a testament to her meticulous plans and Finny's infectious enthusiasm, had indeed consumed them both. But in the quiet moments between bunting battles and engine calculations, she felt the same yearning, a desire for a space just for them, away from the village's manic energy.
"You're right, Finny," she admitted, a blush creeping onto her cheeks. "We need a breather, a chance to just be us, not the Spudnik team or the Ballymuckmore beautification squad."
A mischievous glint danced in Finny's eyes. "Then what do you say, Aoife Spudnik Queen, to a little escape? City lights, a day away from potato-powered mayhem. Just you and me."
Aoife, her laughter echoing like wind chimes in the transformed village, grinned. "City lights? You sure you can handle the bright lights after all this spectacular glow?"
"Ah, Aoife," Finny teased, pulling her close, "city lights got nothin' on the sparkle in your eyes."

The plan was hatched in hushed whispers, a secret escape from the village's grand preparations. A borrowed car, a map with more scribbles than directions, and a backpack filled with dreams and one Agnes' spud pies (just in case) – these were their provisions for a journey beyond the bog, a chance to rediscover the quiet magic of their connection.

As the sun rose above the horizon, bathing the village in its warm glow, Aoife and Finny slipped quietly away. The city lights, distant promises on the horizon, beckoned.

Ballymuckmore, their beloved village, would be waiting for them, its lunacy and laughter undimmed. But for now, they would chase their own celestial dream, a love story written in city lights and the whispered promise of a future filled with adventures, both grand and small.

Finny stepped out of the car, his eyes wide as saucers, like a startled barn owl under a city spotlight. The bustling streets pulsed with an energy he had never imagined, a symphony of honking horns, flashing lights, and a million conversations woven into the urban fabric. The sheer scale of it, the towering, steel-clad giants scraping the sky, left him speechless.

Since arriving in Ballymuckmore from the city as a young lad, he'd stayed firmly stuck in the bog, avoiding a confrontation with painful memories.

Aoife, watching his jaw drop, felt a pang of affection and amusement. This Finny, this wide-eyed wonder with city dust sprinkled on his freckles, was a side of him she hadn't seen before. The boy from the bog, usually so full of mischief and potato-powered bravado, was humbled by the urban cacophony, yet captivated by its undeniable magic.

They spent the day hand-in-hand, navigating the concrete jungle. They devoured exotic dishes that resembled nothing Finny had ever seen in Agnes's kitchen, each bite an explosion of unfamiliar flavours. Aoife, the seasoned city dweller, became his guide, translating the urban hieroglyphics, explaining the neon whispers of advertisements, and introducing him to the hidden gems tucked away in bustling alleys.

They wandered through museums filled with whispered stories of the past, each brushstroke and ancient artefact, a portal to another world. They laughed until their stomachs ached in a brightly lit comedy club, the city's laughter weaving seamlessly with their own.

And as the day surrendered to the velvet embrace of night, they found themselves on a rooftop, the city sprawled beneath them like a glittering constellation. The moon, no longer a familiar companion from the bog, was a distant diamond in the urban sky. Yet, in Aoife's eyes, Finny found a universe of warmth, a familiar moonbeam in the concrete jungle.

The city lights twinkled like a million fireflies trapped in glass jars, painting the faces of Finny and Aoife with a kaleidoscope of colours. They sat on a rooftop bar, their hands intertwined, the city sprawled beneath them, a far cry from the familiar expanse of Ballymuckmore bog. The noise, once overwhelming, now hummed a lullaby, a backdrop to the quiet symphony of their hearts. Love, nurtured in the quiet moments between bunting battles and spudnik calculations, had blossomed under the harsh fluorescent glow of the city.

"Never thought I'd see the day I'd be sipping fancy cocktails overlooking skyscrapers," Finny breathed, swirling the ice in his glass. "Feels like I'm in one of Agnes's far-fetched stories."

Aoife chuckled, her fiery hair catching the city's glow. "And you, the potato-loving, spudnik-building dreamer, in a suit and tie."

Finny grinned, tugging at his tie self-consciously. "Just blending in, Aoife. But the suit doesn't change the dreamer inside. Just gives him a bit more polished ambition, maybe."
They fell silent for a moment, lost in the symphony of city sounds. Then, Aoife spoke, her voice soft but determined. "Five years, Finny. Where do you see yourself?"
Finny raised an eyebrow, surprised by the question. "Honestly? Still in Ballymuckmore, I suppose. Maybe a bigger shed for tinkering, Spudnik 2.0 soaring through the sky... the usual."
Aoife smiled, her eyes filled with a mixture of affection and challenge. "And what about your dreams beyond spudniks and bigger sheds? Remember that lad who used to spend hours drawing fantastical machines?"
Finny felt a blush creep up his neck. "That was years ago, Aoife. Just childhood fancies."
"Fancies that led you to build a potato-powered rocket, Finny. What if you gave those dreams a chance? This city, with its engineers and inventors, could be the fuel you need."
Finny considered her words, the city lights seeming to whisper possibilities. "But Ballymuckmore... it's home. My family, the bog, the smell of peat smoke... it's in my blood now."
Aoife squeezed his hand gently. "Home doesn't have to be a place, Finny. It can be the people you carry in your heart, the dreams you chase. You can be a Ballymuckmore boy and a city dreamer, both at the same time."
Finny looked at her, the city lights reflected in his eyes. Maybe, just maybe, Aoife was right. Maybe the bog and the skyscrapers weren't mutually exclusive. Maybe, in five years, he could be building Spudnik 3.0 with Ballymuckmore pride, fuelled by the city's innovation and his own unyielding spirit. First though, he had some personal demons that needed

vanquishing and that was a bigger undertaking than building a potcheen powered space rocket.

"Maybe you're onto something, Aoife," he said, a slow smile spreading across his face. "Maybe Ballymuckmore's dreamiest spud-slinger can find his place among the city lights too."

They raised their glasses, a toast to dreams, to possibilities, and to the uncharted map of their futures. The city shimmered around them, a canvas waiting to be painted with the stories of a Ballymuckmore boy and his dreams, taking flight, potato-powered or not.

"I never thought I'd like it back here," Finny admitted, his voice barely a whisper, "but with you..." He trailed off, the unfinished sentence a confession etched in the cityscape reflected in his eyes.

Aoife, her heart overflowing, leaned in, their lips meeting under the watchful gaze of the city lights. The kiss, sweet and alive, was a promise whispered in the urban breeze, a pact between two souls who had found their own constellation in the chaos.

Their city escape was a mere blip on the radar of Ballymuckmore's grand preparations, but the ripples it created in their hearts would forever alter the landscape of their relationship. Their day over, they reluctantly returned to the bog with a renewed glow, the love kindled under the city lights adding a new dimension to their bond. Aoife, the spudnik queen, still held the village's lunacy in her palm, but now, her fingers were intertwined with Finny's, a grounding tether in the storm.

Ballymuckmore, its bunting fluttering in the wind, welcomed them back with open arms and stories of the village's exploits. But beside the celebrations and cosmic cheers, Finny and Aoife knew their own adventure had just begun. The city lights, a memory etched in their laughter, were a reminder that their love, like their village, could thrive in any soil, whether bog-soaked or bathed in neon glow. For even in the most unlikely corners, under the watchful gaze of stars or glittering skyscrapers, love has a way of taking root, and growing, wild and beautiful, like a potato flower blooming on a rooftop.

Bog Crater

Aoife burst into Agnes's Pub, a whirlwind of windblown hair and clutched papers. "Sorry I'm late, lads," she panted, dumping the papers onto a table with a mountain-like thud. "Conscience attack, the worst kind."
The spudnik team, already tucking in to another breakfast masterpiece from Agnes' kitchen, exchanged bewildered glances. Sheebie took a cautious sip of her tea. "Conscience attack, you say? Did it bite you or something?"
Aoife, collapsing onto the bench with a groan, shook her head. "Worse. It made me realise we can't just launch Spudnik into the void, hoping for the best! What if it comes plummeting back down on our beloved village, a potato-shaped crater 'n all?"
A collective gasp rippled through the group. The very thought of Spudnik returning as a celestial spud-splosion sent shivers down even Leaky's usually unflappable spine.
"But no launch?" Finny's voice cracked, the echo of disappointment hanging heavy in the air. "This was supposed to be our crowning masterpiece of lunacy! Spudnik, dancing among the stars, a testament to our glorious Ballymuckmoreness!"
Aoife held up a hand, a glint of mischief battling the seriousness in her eyes. "Hold your horses, Finny. I'm not saying no launch, just a launch with a bit more... sanity. "
Mention of the 'S' word drew strange looks from her friends sat round the table.
"Spudnik deserves a proper send-off, not a one-way ticket to oblivion."
She unfolded the mountain of papers, revealing a maze of calculations and diagrams. "We need control, lads. Control

over how it goes up, and most importantly, where it comes down. And I've got just the spot."

She pointed to a map, a finger tracing a circle in the middle of the bog. "Right here. Far enough away from the village to avoid any accidental house demolitions, and close enough for us to witness its glorious return."

Leaky, ever the tinkerer, grumbled, his face a thundercloud. "But Aoife, where's the fun in that? Ballymuckmore lunacy thrives on the unpredictable, the potato-powered chaos! A controlled landing in the bog? That's as exciting as watching paint dry! And trust me, I've seen a lot of paint drying lately."

Aoife leaned closer, her voice dropping to a conspiratorial whisper. "Leaky, my wonderful, distilled friend, think about your shed. Think about the delicate gears, the intricate contraptions. Think about what might happen if Spudnik decided to pay it a visit on its descent."

Leaky's eyes widened, his face morphing from thundercloud to one of panic. The image of his beloved shed, flattened by a celestial spud, was enough to send even the most ardent lunacy enthusiast running for the hills, or rather, the bog.

With a sheepish grin, he conceded. "Alright, alright, Aoife. You win. Controlled landing it is. But if that spud even thinks about straying a millimetre…"

Aoife chuckled, slapping him on the back. "Don't worry, Leaky. We'll have Spudnik back safe and sound, ready for a hero's welcome. Just think, lads, a controlled landing, a proper Irish celebration, and the entire universe watching our little village reach for the stars. Now that's Ballymuckmore lunacy at its finest, seasoned with a sprinkle of responsibility."

And so, with a newfound focus and a dash of Aoife's serious head, the spudnik team shifted gears. The launch remained on schedule, but the destination changed. The bog, once a symbol of quiet solitude, became a landing pad for celestial dreams. The preparations continued, kindled by laughter, lunacy, and a newfound respect for the power of a controlled potato-powered spaceship.

There was just one little issue to be dealt with, explained Aoife. "How do we slow it down from supersonic speeds?"

Aoife's pronouncement about Spudnik's fiery descent hung heavy in the air, a potato-shaped weight on everyone's chest. The bog, once a haven of tranquil mud baths and pebble skipping, now loomed as a potential crater waiting to happen. Hundreds of miles per hour? Leaky, ever the pragmatist, let out a low whistle that could have summoned a banshee.

Finny, his usual bright optimism dimmed, slumped in his seat. "So, what now, Aoife? We can't just let Spudnik become a celestial spud-bomb."

Aoife, however, wasn't one to wallow in potato-based despair. Her eyes, usually sparkling with mischief, now held a steely glint of determination. "We need a parachute, a big one, strong enough to slow that celestial spud down to a gentle bog-plop."

But finding a parachute in Ballymuckmore, especially one big enough to handle Spudnik's celestial aspirations, was as easy as finding a leprechaun with a dry sense of humour. Supplies were scarce, desperation was high, and the air was thick with the aroma of Agnes's sausages and bacon.

Just when the spudnik team seemed on the verge of a collective potato-brained meltdown, Sheebie, her unusually quiet eyes twinkling with their resident mischief, leaned forward. "Leave it to me," she declared, her voice carrying the weight of a thousand potato-sized secrets. "I've got an idea, a plan so cunning it would make a fox blush."

Her words were met with a mix of skepticism and hopeful curiosity. Finny, ever the optimist, perked up. "Spill it, Sheebie! What's your cunning plan?"
But Sheebie, with a sly smile playing on her lips, simply shook her head. "Secrets, Finny, secrets. All will be revealed on launch day, when Spudnik descends from the heavens, not as a fiery meteor, but as a gentle plop, thanks to yours truly."

Customs Still Searching

Ballymuckmore, adorned in its rainbow finery, buzzed with the nervous excitement of judging day. Tourists wandered, cameras at the ready, capturing the village's bizarre beauty. The bunting and sheep-shaped flowerpots aside, a different kind of drama unfolded.

At the launchpad, a motley crew of spudnik enthusiasts watched as three black cars, ominous as crows against the cerulean sky, pulled up outside the Pub with No Name. The air crackled with a tension that had nothing to do with impending judgment. These were the men from Customs and Excise, sworn enemies of Zorg, the potcheen maestro, and they had finally caught his scent.

Zorg, always one step ahead of the law and two steps behind common sense, was at Mission Control, his face as weathered as a spud skin left in the sun too long. Turns out, twenty years of moonlighting as Ireland's greatest unofficial distiller had accumulated a hefty duty bill, a sum that could choke a bullfrog.

Sheebie checked that the door was shut, no point advertising their presence. She turned back to Zorg. The newspaper he had been holding floated slowly to the floor. The only door to mission control was still firmly closed.

As quickly as he arrived, Zorg had vanished, a wisp of smoke against the potato-dotted landscape. The legend that he was, once more just a whisper on the wind.

The Customs men, however, were less adept at disappearing acts. They stalked through the village, their beady eyes searching for the telltale glint of a still and the pungent aroma of fermented spuds.

Meanwhile, the spudnik crew, their faces grim, huddled around the launchpad. The fuel for Spudnik's celestial voyage? Pure, unadulterated potcheen, Zorg's finest vintage. Leaky's shed, now a potential crime scene, housed the key to their dreams – and the Customs men's ultimate prize.

Panicked whispers filled the air, thick as potato soup. They needed a distraction, a diversion so audacious, so Ballymuckmore, that it would send the law hounds on a wild goose chase. Sheebie, her eyes glinting with their usual mischief, stepped forward, armed with a Ballymuckmore sized grin and a toolbox full of spanners.

"Leave it to me," she declared, her voice carrying the weight of a thousand hair-brained schemes. "Operation Mirage is a go!" Sheebie, ever the mastermind, hatched a plan as cunning as a leprechaun with a pot of gold. She armed the village's teenagers, a band of mischievous bog goblins disguised as innocent youths, with spanners and screwdrivers. Their mission? A grand sign-swap, a symphony of redirection.

In a whirlwind of laughter and clattering metal, the village's signposts were transformed. Signs intended to point tourists and judges to Ballymuckmore's wonderful attractions, now led anywhere but and all roads pointed away from the Leaky's shed.

Ballymuckmore became a labyrinth of whimsical lies, sending the Customs men on a wild goose chase through fields of giggling sheep and down meandering bog paths that led nowhere.

They chased Seamus the donkey in circles, mistook a pile of spuds for a still, and ended up in the Pub with No Name, their faces buried in steaming bowls of potato stew.

The problem hadn't gone away, but for now they were more interested in Agnes' culinary delights than where the arch villain Zorg could be found.

Disaster averted, at least for now, work continue getting Spudnik ready to make its grand entrance.

Bonanza, usually a haven of bubbling stew and potato-powered tinkering, became a cacophony of metal groans and Leaky's anguished cries. A sickening thud had echoed from deep within, the sound of Spudnik's meticulously crafted hatch tearing itself free, taking their celestial dreams with it. The parachute, carefully tucked away like a sleeping pup, was now exposed, its drogue hanging uselessly. Disaster, thick as Agnes's potato soup, clung to the air.

Panic engulfed the crew, their hopes disappearing faster than a balloon on a windy day. Without the hatch, Spudnik would be a celestial bomb, destined to leave a crater in bog. Leaky, his face as pale as a peeled potato, wrung his hands, muttering about gears and physics.

But from the depths of Ballymuckmore's lunacy rose Finny, the village optimist armed with a scrap of paper in one hand and a grin as wide as the bog on the other. "Don't you worry, lads," he declared, his voice a beacon of hope. "I've got this."

With a wink and a mischievous glint in his eyes, he disappeared into the village, clutching a paper with the dimensions of the required hatch. Where he was headed, nobody dared ask. Ballymuckmore had been stripped bare, its every pot, pan, and rusty shed door repurposed for Spudnik's celestial journey.

Finny reappeared a while later, a triumphant grin lighting up his face. In his outstretched hands, he held a metal panel, its triangular shape and size a perfect match for Spudnik's gaping wound. Sheebie took one look at it and burst into laughter. "Only you, Finny," she chuckled, shaking her head in disbelief. We don't have any paint left, so it'll have to go on as it is. Meanwhile, at the top of the neighbouring valley, the car containing Fiona O'Flannery, Seamus MacNamara and Bridget Malone, the judges was making its way to the next village on the list of competitors.

"Kilmuckety should be the next turning on the right" Fiona was the navigator, "It should be signposted"

There was a large road sign clearly showing Ballymuckmore to the left. Where you would find yourself should you turn right, was a mystery. Instead of the village name, there was a large triangular void.

Day of Reckoning

Constable O'Toole, his chest puffed with a pride that rivalled Agnes's pastry, marched at the head of the procession, a crisp uniform a stark contrast to the village's vibrant chaos. His task: to guide the three Beautiful Ireland competition judges, a trio as mismatched as a plate of Seamus's leftovers, through the sun splashed streets of Ballymuckmore.

The judges, Fiona O'Flannery with her camera perpetually poised, Seamus MacNamara with a twinkle in his eye and a beard that could house a family of leprechauns, and Bridget Malone with her floral-patterned dress clashing gloriously with the rainbow bunting, were bombarded with smiles and friendly greetings. Every villager, from Leaky in his patched overalls to Agnes in her Sunday apron (though it sported a suspicious potato-shaped stain), had donned their best church clothes, looking like a motley crew ready for a celestial ceili.

Adding to the pandemonium was a local TV crew, their cameras whirring like overexcited bumblebees. "Live from Ballymuckmore," the reporter boomed, his voice echoing through the narrow streets. "It's a beautiful day in this quirky village, folks, and the competition is fierce!"

Fierce it might have been, but Ballymuckmore's brand of competition was all about the craic, the lunacy, the sheer joy of living in a village where a potato powered rocket was the pièce de résistance. The judges, initially bewildered by the cacophony of singing sheep, potato-powered bicycles, and Seamus's enthusiastic recitation of ancient bog myths, were soon swept up in the infectious laughter and warmth.

Fiona captured the twinkle in Leaky's eyes as he explained the intricate workings of his strange contraptions, her camera clicking like a castanet in a jig. Seamus, beard bristling with delight, continued to regale Bridget with tales of bog fairies, his voice weaving magic into the air. Bridget, in turn, pointed out the beauty of wildflowers growing in the most unexpected places, her floral dress mirroring the vibrant chaos around them.

Constable O'Toole, initially nervous about keeping the judges away from the launchpad, soon found himself chuckling along with them. He watched as they, led by a mischievous Finny, tried their hand at pebble skipping, their dignified poses dissolving into laughter. He saw the judges, no longer just visitors, but honorary members of Ballymuckmore's madcap family, sharing stories and potato-shaped smiles with the villagers.

The sun, an orb dipped in honey, cast a warm glow on Ballymuckmore, but Constable O'Toole's forehead felt like a freshly-dug bog, beaded with nervous sweat. Everything, for once, was going to plan. The judges, Fiona with her sun-kissed camera, Seamus with his beard of moss and Bridget with her flower-power dress, were beaming. The villagers were regaling the judges with stories of uniquely powered tractors and potato-shaped UFO sightings. The TV crew, their microphones buzzing like hungry bees, were capturing it all.

But Ballymuckmore wouldn't be Ballymuckmore without a dash of chaos, a sprinkle of lunacy. And as if summoned by the collective mischievous grin of the village, the day took a turn into the realm of the absurd.

Firstly, there was the sheep. A gate, left open by a wide-eyed tourist, became the gateway to a floral apocalypse. The sheep, a woolly whirlwind, charged through the village, munching their way through meticulously crafted displays like miniature lawnmowers powered by daisies. Petunias became appetisers, pansies main courses, and Seamus's prize-winning sunflowers, dessert. The judges, initially aghast, soon found themselves doubled over with laughter as Fiona captured the scene, her camera clicking like a frantic castanet.

Then, as if on cue, the dreaded Customs men reappeared. Having devoured Agnes's potato stew (and half the village's gossip) in record time, they were back on the hunt for the elusive Zorg and his magical still.

But the pièce de résistance, the grand finale of Ballymuckmore's lunacy, arrived in the form of Seamus the donkey. Freed from his tether by a mischievous Finny, Seamus, nostrils twitching was on the hunt for a personal buffet, Bridget's floral-patterned dress.

The arrival of the Customs men coinciding with the sheep-induced floral carnage, was like a splash of vinegar in a bowl of potato soup. The villagers, faces etched with a mix of amusement and apprehension, scattered like startled rabbits, as they did so, Seamus saw his quarry.

Bridget stood there, like a matador, defiant in the eyes of a great bull. Seamus, his hooves slipping on the smooth cobblestones, as if pawing the ground.

Before anybody could say Ballymuckmore, Bridget, shrieking like a startled robin, found herself chased across the village, her flower-power dress billowing like a sail in a gale.

The TV crew, their faces lit up with glee, captured the pandemonium with gusto. The camera zoomed in on Seamus's determined munching, Fiona's lens catching Bridget's comical escape, and the microphone, held by a breathless reporter, recorded the soundtrack of laughter, bleating sheep, and Agnes's admonishing shouts.

Constable O'Toole, his initial panic replaced by a resigned chuckle, watched the chaos unfold. This wasn't just a judging anymore, it was a performance, a live potato-powered reality show starring the entire village. And as Seamus, finally sated by a mouthful of daisies, sauntered off, Bridget, her dress a tattered masterpiece, joined the judges in a fit of laughter that echoed across the bog.

The launchpad, still shrouded in secrecy, waited for its grand unveiling, but for now, Ballymuckmore basked in the afterglow of its own unique brand of lunacy. The judges, their eyes sparkling with more than just the sun's reflection, had witnessed the village's soul, its chaotic heart that beat to the rhythm of laughter, sheep, and lofty dreams. And as the cameras clicked and the sheep continued their floral feast, one thing was certain: Ballymuckmore, the village that would dare to paint the cosmos Satin Butterscotch, had already won. They might not have won the competition, but they had won the hearts of the judges, the viewers, and even the sheep. And that, in Ballymuckmore, was a victory sweeter than any potato pie.

Blessed be Spudnik

Finny's face was the colour of a sunburnt spud on a scorcher of a day. Spudnik, the celestial dream, stood resplendent on the launchpad, ready to paint the Milky Way Satin Butterscotch. Everything was in place, fuel tanks bubbling, dials whirring, Seamus the sheepdog even sporting his lucky collar. But one crucial element was missing: the holy blessing of Father Dougal.
"Saints preserve us, Finny!" Sheebie wrung her hands, her voice a lamenting wind. "We can't send Spudnik to meet St. Bridget without a proper send-off from Father Dougal!"
Panic gnawed at Finny. Father Dougal, ever the elusive soul, seemed to have vanished into the thin air of prelaunch excitement. Tourists swarmed the bog, ufologists with tinfoil hats pointed frantically at the sky, and Beautiful Ireland competition judges tripped over hay bales, their floral dresses still in tatters from the unwanted attention from a certain donkey, who will remain nameless. You know who it was, anyway..
"Right then, lads and lasses, Operation: Find Father Dougal is a go!" Finny rallied the village youth, a swarm of children armed with magnifying glasses and shrieks of "Father Dougal, where are ya?" They scoured the village, checking behind Agnes's prize-winning turnips, peeking into every dusty corner, even braving the dreaded turf toilet – all to no avail.
Reports trickled in: "Found Finny's lucky shamrock, but no Father Dougal!" "Spotted Seamus chasing sheep near Mrs. O'Leary's fence, but no sign of the holy man!" Finny felt his potato heart sink faster than a tourist in the bog.
Just as despair threatened to drown the bog in a wave of tears, a triumphant shout pierced the air. It was young Mickey, eyes

wide with the thrill of discovery, pointing towards the church graveyard. There, Father Dougal sat, engaged in a lively theological debate with Agnes's prize-winning rooster, Seamus, perched on one of the gravestones.

Getting Father Dougal to Spudnik was another saga in itself. Every step was punctuated by a villager accosting him: "Father, could you bless my new spud-peeling knife?" "Father, my cousin in Galway needs your advice on curing a case of the dancing turnips!" "Father, tell us again about the time you almost convinced the Queen to visit Ballymuckmore for the annual Sheep Shearing Festival!"

Finny turned to apologise to the villagers that Father Dougal had an urgent appointment he couldn't miss. When Finny looked back, Father Dougal was gone. "Not again!" He scanned the area. He soon found him, inspecting the spinster Maguires petunias.

"Aren't they looking lovely"

"Yes, Father, but if you wouldn't mind, we are a little pushed for time." Finny tried not to let his frustration get the better of him.

"A christening was it ?"

"No, Father, a blessing before a long journey"

"Ah, yes, I remember now. You and that nice O'Rouke girl. Will you be gone long?"

Finally, they reached Bonanza and Finny showed the good Father in through the side door.

"And where is the thing you wish me to bless ?"

The crew all turned to look at Spudnik. The good Father turned to match their gaze. Slowly his head tilted back. A little at first, but then more until Sheebie thought he would fall over backwards.

Father Dougal stared at the monster rocket, his jaw dropping lower than Seamus chasing a runaway sausage. A silent "Blimey" slipped past his lips, a testament to the sight that would have shocked even the most jaded saint.
Finny nudged him gently. "Just a quick blessing, Father, then we're off to space!"
"Space you say. Lovely"
Father Dougal cleared his throat, his eyes still trying to take in the sight before him.
"Has the rocket got name?"
"Yes, it's called Spudnik" Finny responded proudly.
Raising his hands, he boomed, "May the Almighty God guide, er, Spudnik on its journey, may its engine roar with the wrath of a hungry sheepdog and its course be straight and true! Amen!"
Spudnik, baptised in a shower of blessings and laughter, was ready to take flight. Finny, his face now the colour of a happy boiled spud, grinned at Father Dougal.
"That'll do, Father. That'll do nicely."
Father Dougal could be heard muttering under his breath as he left "A Rocket, a real live rocket. Going to have make some changes to my sermon. A Rocket !"

Are Ewe Dancing

The final leg of the tour, Bonanza, loomed like a beacon in the fading light. The judges, their faces flushed with laughter and the lingering scent of Agnes's potato stew, followed Constable O'Toole with an eagerness that rivalled a hungry pig. They were eager, finally, to lay eyes on the pièce de résistance, the celestial spud that promised to launch Ballymuckmore into the annals of legend.

But as they neared the field housing Bonanza, a wrench was thrown into the well-oiled gears of destiny. The hose attached to the potcheen fuelling valve, the very lifeblood of Spudnik's journey, refused to budge. Stuck fast, it threatened to ground their dreams faster than a boot stuck in the bog.

Panic threatened to engulf the room, a cold sweat clinging to Leaky's brow like a second potato skin. But Ballymuckmore, the village where lunacy was as common as puddles, was not one to surrender to mere mechanical hiccups. Time to buy some time in typical style.

Enter Sheebie and Seamus, the sheepdog (not to be confused with Seamus, the donkey, who was currently enjoying a post-floral feast in Agnes's garden). With a mischievous glint in their eyes and a wagging tail that could propel a rocket, they launched into an impromptu sheepdog trial of epic proportions. Forget your run-of-the-mill fetching and herding. This was Ballymuckmore, where sheep weren't just barnyard beasts, but celestial collaborators. The woolly flock, spurred on by Sheebie's whistles and Seamus's enthusiastic barks, formed intricate shapes that would put even the most seasoned artist to shame. Circles, squares, even a heart shape, the sheep danced across the hay bales, their hooves tapping a rhythm that had the judges humming along.

Then, in a moment of pure lunacy that would make even the most seasoned potato-loving leprechaun chuckle, the sheep, under Sheebie's masterful guidance, began to dance. Yes, dance. Their little hooves, adorned with makeshift bells, clicked and clacked on the wooden stage, a flock of baa-lerinas, a chorus of rhythm that sent the judges into fits of laughter.

As the judges, their faces stained with tears of mirth, watched the sheep's tapping ballet, the worry about the stuck valve faded into the background. For in that moment, they witnessed the true spirit of Ballymuckmore – a village where even the most mundane could be transformed into a spectacle of joy, where laughter flowed like potcheen and dreams danced on the hooves of sheep.

And so, while Leaky and Finny tinkered away at the valve, the judges, their hearts full of Ballymuckmore's magic, watched the sheep tap their way into the annals of village legend. The launch might be delayed, but the spirit of Ballymuckmore, its lunacy and its laughter, had soared higher than any Spudnik ever could.

A collective breath held in Bonanza as Leaky, with a final, resounding blow from his mighty hammer, freed the stubborn potcheen hose. It sprang loose with a hiss, the sound almost a sigh of relief from the team.

There was no time to lose as they made their way to Mission Control. Sheebie snuck away from the stage show, leaving Seamus to steal the limelight as he directed the sheep in one final outrageous dance routine.

Switches were thrown and dials turned as Aoife reached the control panel, her eyes ablaze with celestial fire, launched into a series of rapid-fire checks.

"Fuel?" she barked, her voice echoing through the hay-bale-lined space.

"Fuel is Go, lass!" roared Leaky, a wide grin splitting his potato-peeling-stained face.

"Comms?"

"Comms are Go!" Finny chimed in, his grin almost matching Leaky's.

The tension crackled in the air, not unlike the electricity sparking across the circuits of Spudnik's hidden belly.

Everyone present, from the judges beaming with anticipation to the TV crew buzzing with excitement, knew this was it. The finale, the moment Ballymuckmore would show the world what it was made of and in which colour.

Aoife threw a switch in the Mission Control room and a large countdown clock was illuminated, clearly visible above the leprechaun on Bonanza's colourful exterior.

With a flourish, Finny hit the button marked 'Sesame' and after a short, nervous pause, the massive side doors of Bonanza majestically swung open, revealing a tantalising glimpse of Satin Butterscotch glory.

There was a collective gasp from the crowd.

Spudnik, sleek and gleaming under the setting sun, was no longer just a whispered dream but a tangible reality.

The TV crew, sensing a moment for the history books, scrambled, informing their studios.

Network logos across the globe flickered, switching to the live feed from the heart of boggy Ireland. Spudnik was going global.

As the assembled masses joined in counting down the final numbers, a booming voice shattered the celestial anticipation.

"Stop what you're doing!"

The words rang out, heavy as a rain-soaked ewe, from the doorway. And there, bathed in the dying light, stood the dreaded Customs men. Their faces grim, reflecting the storm clouds gathering on the horizon.

For a moment, silence choked the air, thicker than the bog mud after a downpour. The countdown clock, mockingly bright, blinked a tantalising 00:10. Ballymuckmore's dreams, Spudnik's celestial journey, hung precariously in the balance. Would the village of lunacy and potcheen power defy the forces of bureaucracy? Or would the Customs men, driven by the sour scent of duty and the clinking of coppers, clip Spudnik's celestial wings even before they could unfurl?

The answer, dear reader, lies in the wind rustling through the bog, in the glint of mischief in Sheebie's eyes, and in the potato-powered ingenuity that pulsed through the very heart of Ballymuckmore. Stay tuned, for the finale of Spudnik's tale promises to be as absurd, as exhilarating, and as quintessentially Ballymuckmore as the village itself.

Fly Spudnik, Fly

The Customs men descended upon Mission Control and Bonanza like a swarm of angry wasps, their faces contorted with bureaucratic fury. Accusations of illegal potcheen production and celestial smuggling filled the air, bouncing off the hay bales and echoing through the stunned silence. Permits, licenses, and regulations were brandished like potato-shaped weapons, threatening to smother the Spudnik crew's dreams in a mountain of paperwork.
Constable O'Toole, ever the defender of Ballymuckmore's lunacy, stepped forward, his voice a lone potato in the storm. "Hold on a minute, lads!" he boomed, his uniform puffing out in defiance. "What jurisdiction do you have over grain silos? Last I checked, this wasn't a distillery, it was a granary!"
The Customs men, momentarily stunned by O'Toole's question, faltered. Their bureaucratic arsenal, honed for pubs and back alleys, seemed ill-equipped for this curveball. They sputtered and stammered, citing regulations and procedures, but their words lacked the conviction of a man facing a potato-powered rocket.
"This, this contraption is being used to store illegal liquor and it's being impounded" The chief Customs man spluttered.
"What, this big Satin Butterscotch Spud Rocket?" enquired the Constable.
"A rocket, you say. Er... you need a permit to fly anything above four hundred feet off the ground" The customs man grinned, like the cat that had got the cream. He wasn't sure where he remembered that from, but it was a real regulation. "Nothing is to be touched until the relevant department has been informed. We'll be back with the proper authority, and

then, laddies, your little spud-bomb will be grounded faster than a rabbit in a potato patch."

The men in suits walked the spudnik team from the launchpad, their chins almost scraping the ground. Their dream, just like Bridget's floral dress, in tatters.

The threat hung heavy in the air, a huge storm cloud threatening to rain on Ballymuckmore's parade. But Sheebie, ever the master of mischief, saw an opportunity in the chaos. With a sly wink at Leaky and a barely audible whistle, she gave Seamus, the sheepdog, his instructions.

Seamus, no stranger to his mistress's whims, understood the gravity of the situation. The fate of Spudnik, the celestial spud, rested on his furry shoulders. With a determined bark that would have made a leprechaun proud, he darted between the legs of the flustered Customs men, a streak of black and white fur against the hay bales.

He hurtled towards Mission Control, masterfully avoiding the flailing arms of the Customs men. The team could see him through the window as he jumped up on the main instrument desk.

Seamus stood tall, his eyes fixed on the red button that pulsed like a potato-powered heart.

And then, with a huge sheepdog grin and a mighty bark that echoed across the launchpad and shook every window in the village, Seamus did what no one expected, but everybody hoped. He planted his paw on the red button, pushing it down with all his might.

The world held its breath. The countdown clock, which had been mockingly frozen at 00:10, sprung back to life, its numbers flashing like fireflies in the fading light.

The Customs men around the launchpad ran for cover.

A collective gasp escaped the Spudnik crew as the engine roared to life, the potcheen-fuelled flames licking at the ground.

Spudnik, the celestial spud, trembled on its launchpad, its voice ringing out across the village. The Customs men, faces contorted in a mixture of shock and outrage, watched as their authority dissolved in the face of Ballymuckmore's lunacy.

The world around Bonanza was obscured in a symphony of flame and fury. The potato-powered engine roared with a symphony of pops and hisses, the flames licking at the launchpad like eager tongues. The ground trembled with the Spudnik's heartbeat, the air thick with the smell of burnt hay and potato-infused exhaust.

Then, slowly, almost reluctantly, the Butterscotch behemoth began to move. As if pulling itself out by its finger tips, first a hand, then a foot and before long a yard, the hopes and dreams of a village inching its way out of the belly of Bonanza .

With each agonising crawl, a collective gasp rose from the crowd, hearts pounding against ribs like frantic fish.

Finally, in a burst of glory that bathed the bog in Satin Butterscotch hues, Spudnik fully emerged.

"Ah, that's where Kilmuckety is!" Fiona O'Flannery exclaimed, as the unpainted triangular panel revealed itself.

It rose, majestically, like a Satin Butterscotch phoenix reborn from the ashes of bureaucracy. The wind whistled around its hull, a celestial symphony playing in harmony with the notes of the engine. Mission Control, dwarfed by the beautiful behemoth, shrank into a speck on the bog, a testament to the village's audacious dream.

And suddenly, it was real. Spudnik, the village's lunacy made manifest, was no longer just wishful thinking. It was a potato-shaped reality, hurtling towards the heavens, carrying with it the hopes and dreams of a village that dared to paint the cosmos Satin Butterscotch.

In that moment, everything else faded. The flustered Customs men, their bureaucratic bluster drowned out by the rocket's roar. The judges, their faces beaming with a childlike awe. Even the sheep, momentarily frozen in a state of wonder.

All eyes were on Spudnik, the celestial spud, as it pierced the twilight sky, its potato-fuelled trail a luminous scar against the velvety darkness. Ballymuckmore, the village of lunatics and dreamers, had launched their beloved spud into the cosmos, proving that even the most absurd dreams could take flight, powered by laughter, ingenuity, and a healthy dose of chaos.

In the whirlwind of chaos and potato-fuelled fumes, the Spudnik crew, nimble as a trout, slipped past the spluttering Customs men and dashed into mission control. There, in the middle of a tangle of wires and gauges, they huddled around the monitors, watching with bated breath as their celestial spud danced towards the stars.

Dials whirred, lights blinked, and numbers scrolled across the screens, each one a testament to the village's lunacy and Zorg's potato-powered genius. But the number that held their gaze captive, the number that pulsed like a cosmic heart, was the altitude.

Fifty-one miles... Fifty-two... Fifty-three... inching closer to the celestial prize: space.

The air in the cramped control centre was thick with anticipation, a heady mix of fear and exhilaration. Sheebie, her lips moving in silent prayer, clutched Seamus, who barked excitedly at the twinkling tapestry of stars on the monitor. Finny, his face a canvas of grins, bounced on the balls of his feet, barely able to contain his potato-powered glee.

And then, as the altimeter ticked over to sixty-two miles, a hush fell over the room. Aoife, Mission Control herself, her eyes gleaming with tears of triumph, reached out and gently nudged the red kill switch. With a sputter and a cough, the potcheen-fuelled engine fell silent, the roar replaced by a breathtaking stillness.

Ballymuckmore had done it. They had defied the authorities, embraced the absurd, and launched their celestial spud into the cosmos. They had touched the void, tasted the nectar of space, and painted their potato-shaped dreams across the star-dusted canvas of the universe.

But the cheers, the laughter, the celebratory shots of potcheen – all would have to wait. For the ultimate test, the descent, loomed large. Spudnik, once a fragile dream in the celestial ocean, now faced the treacherous journey back to Earth. With hearts pounding like pistons, the crew turned their attention to the descent controls, a symphony of dials and levers that held the fate of their potato-powered dream in their delicate balance. While the Spudnik crew, running on pure adrenaline and the sheer joy of celestial defiance, grappled with the descent controls, they remained blissfully unaware of the global spectacle they had become. News channels across the world, mouths agape and cameras glued to the sky, tracked Spudnik's every wobble.

CNN, ever the bastion of serious journalism, struggled to maintain its stoic facade. A bespectacled anchor, his brow furrowed like a ploughed field, attempted to impart gravity to the situation. "We are witnessing," he stammered, his voice cracking slightly, "an… unconventional launch from a remote village in Ireland. Experts remain… perplexed. This apparently is a ….. potato-powered spacecraft."

BBC News adopted a more whimsical tone. A bubbly presenter, her smile as bright as a button in the sun, regaled viewers with Ballymuckmore's eccentricities. "Live from the side of a bog!" she chirped, her voice tinged with a hint of Irish lilt. "The folks of Ballymuckmore have done it, folks! They've launched a spud to the stars! Now, I may not know much about astro-navigation, but I do recognise that colour, I've got in my kitchen, I do believe it's Satin Butterscotch"

In Moscow, RT took a more skeptical approach. A stern-faced anchor, his voice heavy with suspicion, questioned the motives behind the launch. "Is this," he intoned, his eyes narrowed, "a covert potato-based weapons test by the West? Are they attempting to colonise the moon,? We urge caution, viewers, and remind you that potatoes were once used by the Great Hunger to… oppress…" Thankfully, his ominous monologue was cut short by a live feed of Seamus, the sheepdog, chasing sheep across the launchpad, sending the studio into fits of laughter.

Governments scrambled, astronomers squinted, and even the Queen of England, bless her potato loving heart, was rumoured to have had a cup of Earl Grey with the telly on, a mischievous twinkle in her eye.

But back in Ballymuckmore, the fate of their celestial spud rested in Sheebie's ingenious hands.

As Spudnik dipped below the five-mile mark, Sheebie, her finger hovering over the crimson switch, took a deep breath. This was it. The moment of truth, the culmination of countless late nights and mugs of potcheen. With a whispered prayer to St. Bridget, the patron saint of lunatics and celestial adventurers, she flipped the switch.

Without any amateur dramatics, the Satin Butterscotch beauty launched its own bundle. It seemed an age as it slowly unfurled. The crowd gasped, Spudnik was still aiming for an unspud like ending in the bog.

Then the air caught the enormous canopy and it filled. Its red and white billowing stripiness rapidly slowing Spudnik. It looked every part like a real NASA space mission, except for one small detail. Well, not actually that small.

Emblazoned across the side of the canopy where the words "O'Rourke's Circus"

"My cousin", smiled Sheebie, "I did tell him I'd get it back to him by Wednesday"

Aoife glanced towards the TV crew. "You can't beat advertising like that"

Relief, sweet and potcheen scented, flooded the room. They had done it. Spudnik, the celestial spud, was returning to Earth, its descent as gentle as a moonbeam bouncing off Agnes's prizewinning turnips.

Under a sky splashed with the remnants of sunset, the Spudnik crew gathered, faces turned upwards, hearts still pounding like pistons. Finny, his grin wider than the bog after a downpour, pointed at the descending spud. Sheebie, silent tears glistening in her eyes, held Seamus close, his tail wagging a celestial symphony. Leaky, his potato-peeling hands clenched, muttered a prayer of thanks to the gods.

And then, in a slow, majestic dance, Spudnik glided towards the welcoming embrace of the bog. The Big Top parachute, a vibrant banner against the twilight sky, guided the potato-shaped wonder gently, a cosmic lullaby hummed by the wind. When Spudnik finally touched down, settling with a soft bounce amongst the reeds, a cheer erupted from the gathered spectators. It was a sound that shook the bog, rattled the windows of Mission Control, and echoed across the fields, a symphony of relief, joy, and the unyielding spirit of a village that dared to paint the cosmos Satin Butterscotch. Ballymuckmore had touched space, tasted the nectar of the stars, and returned to Earth, their hearts full of stardust and their eyes gleaming with the promise of even more lunacy to come. For Spudnik's journey was just the beginning, the first in a ocean waiting to be explored. And as the village gathered around the launchpad, sharing laughter and potato-filled stories under the twilight sky, one thing was certain: Ballymuckmore, the village of dreamers and potato-powered mischief, had cemented its place in the annals of history, not just as potato farmers, but as celestial daredevils who dared to launch their dreams into the cosmos and return, triumphant, to their beloved bog.

The legend of Spudnik, the celestial spud, had only just begun, and as the stars twinkled above, reflecting the glow of a billion potato-shaped hopes, one thing was certain: the sky was no longer the limit, it was just the beginning of Ballymuckmore's potcheen powered adventure.

Epilogue

Let me confess, dear reader, that I never truly believed they'd pull it off. Yet, here I am, holding this weathered manuscript in my hands, a testament to the unwavering spirit of Finny, Aoife, Sheebie, Leaky, and even the sometimes skeptical Seamus (whichever one that may be). They faced down my doubts and the laws of physics (well, maybe bent them a little) to achieve the impossible. It serves as a poignant reminder that even the most audacious dreams can take flight, and that sometimes, the most enchanting journeys begin with nothing more than a potato, a sprinkle of madness, and a whole lot of heart.

For those wondering about the Beautiful Ireland competition, well Ballymuckmore didn't win. However, they were awarded an appropriately coloured rosette in a new category : Village most likely to colonise another planet.

Until next time, from the rolling hills and peat-scented winds of Ballymuckmore,

The Author